Who Am I Without the Trauma? A Journey Back to Yourself

Josiah Cornell

Content Note
This book gently explores themes such as childhood trauma, grief, domestic violence, anxiety, emotional abuse, neurodiversity, and mental health relapse.
While written to validate and support, some content may feel triggering to those still navigating active wounds.
Please go at your own pace. Pause when needed. You are not alone.

Understanding the Brain's Role in Trauma and Mental Health

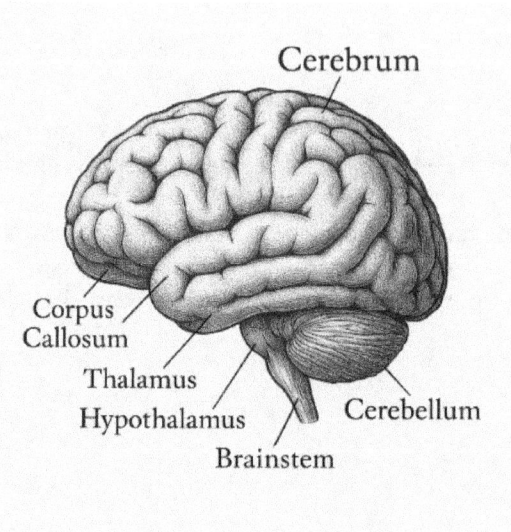

The brain is the command centre for our emotions, thoughts, and survival instincts. Each region plays a distinct role in how we process trauma and navigate mental health challenges.

The amygdala, although not directly labelled here, is housed within the cerebrum and is crucial for detecting threats and triggering the *fight, flight, freeze, or fawn* response, it's often hyperactive in individuals with PTSD and CPTSD, causing heightened fear or emotional reactivity. The thalamus acts as a relay station, filtering sensory input, which can become dysregulated during trauma, amplifying triggers. The hypothalamus regulates stress hormones like cortisol, frequently over activated in those living with chronic anxiety or burnout.

The prefrontal cortex (situated at the front of the cerebrum) governs reasoning and impulse control, yet often "goes offline" during emotional flashbacks or panic. The brainstem maintains basic survival functions, and when trauma is overwhelming, it can anchor the body in a state of constant alertness or shutdown. Together, these regions illustrate that mental health isn't just "in our head" emotionally, it's biologically rooted in the wiring of our brain and nervous system.

Introduction: Behind Closed Doors – Where Mental Health Really Lives

Before We Begin: A Gentle Pause

This is not just a book; it's a heartfelt companion on your journey. It's not designed to be rushed through or read in one sitting, and there are no quick answers to seek here. Instead, it seeks to walk beside you, supporting you at your own pace.

Before we embark on this journey together, I want to share something profoundly important, your permission. Permission to take your time. Permission to pause when needed. Permission to skip ahead and return to a chapter later if it feels too heavy today. Know that this is a space free from judgment, there's no right or wrong way to heal.

As you settle in, perhaps you'd like to make yourself a warm cup of tea or coffee. Step outside for a moment and let the breeze touch your skin. Take a deep breath and ground yourself in the present. Remember, you are not behind; you are exactly where you should be.

Within these pages, you'll discover gentle tools, reflections, and supportive notes. These are not demands placed upon you but invitations to explore at your own pace. This book is here to provide a comforting space, not to overwhelm you.

This is your story, and it unfolds at your rhythm. Nurture it with tenderness. You truly deserve that.

This book was crafted not in isolation, but rather from the rich tapestry of real life; from those moments in the trenches where silence often speaks louder than words, and where healing is often just the courageous act of getting through the next hour. For over seven years, I have immersed myself in the world of criminal justice, navigating emotionally charged environments. I have worked in prisons, where the majority of inmate's grapple with some form of mental health challenge, a stark reminder of our shared human experience. I've been part of frontline Domestic Violence services, witnessing trauma manifest behind closed doors, often unseen and unresolved. I've also served in probation, where mental health struggles frequently lie beneath layers of coping mechanisms and past behaviours, waiting for the right moment to emerge.

Who this book is for?

Whether you're reading this on your best day or in the middle of your darkest one, I want you to know this isn't a textbook, it's a conversation, a comfort, and a companion. Each chapter offers insight, reflection, and space to breathe. There's no pressure to finish it in one sitting. Just take what you need, when you need it.

Through this journey, I've had the privilege of connecting with individuals from all walks of life, those labelled as "offenders," those bravely fleeing abuse, and those striving to rebuild their lives after enduring overwhelming hardship. I've learned something profound: mental health doesn't discriminate. It transcends socioeconomic status, background, and outward appearances and often defies the expectations we may hold.

My passion for this work sparked when I enrolled at South Essex College, where I met a remarkable tutor, Ria Punt. She introduced me to the realms of counselling, mental health, and psychology, illuminating not just the theory, but the humanity behind it. Her guidance transformed my perspective, helping me understand that mental health is not merely an academic subject, it's a deeply personal and often painful journey. Continuing my studies at East London University in Stratford enriched my understanding of these complex topics, solidifying my commitment to make healing more human, accessible, and heartfelt.

However, the most impactful lessons I gained didn't stem from textbooks or classroom lectures. They emerged from lived experiences, listening to stories, offering compassion, and walking alongside someone close to me who fights their own mental health battles daily. So, let me clarify: this book isn't a manual or a quick fix. It's not a glossy self-help guide with simplistic answers. Instead, it's a mirror reflecting the intricate nature of our experiences.

This book speaks to you, the person often seen as the strong one, who feels like they're quietly falling apart inside. It's for the over thinkers who hide their anxiety behind humour, and for those adults still carrying the weight of childhood wounds. It's for those of you who devote yourselves to supporting everyone else but often feel invisible in your own lives.

Together, we will challenge the myths surrounding mental health: that depression can only look like sadness, that anger is inherently negative, and the misleading belief that simply "functioning" means you're okay. The reality is much more nuanced: you can laugh at work while feeling broken inside; you can comfort others while wrestling with your own struggles; you can appear to manage it all while feeling like you're drowning underneath.

Each chapter is thoughtfully crafted to hold space for your pain, your healing, your anger, your numbness, and your survival. This isn't a guide to a perfect life; it's an invitation to start a conversation, one that honours the beautiful messiness of simply being human. If your heart feels heavy, if your mind feels weary, if you find yourself suspended between falling apart and holding it all together, this book is for you.

I don't just talk about mental health; I live it. I wrote this book not to save you, but to walk beside you and say: "I understand. I've been there. You are not alone." Let's wander through these clinical aspects together, and then we'll dive deeper into the rich tapestry of what mental health looks and feels like, especially when no one's watching.

Mental Health in the UK: 2025 Overview

Prevalence and Treatment

Annual Prevalence: Approximately 1 in 4 people in England experience a mental health problem each year.

Weekly Prevalence: About 1 in 6 people report experiencing common mental health issues, such as anxiety or depression, in any given week.

Treatment Access: Only around 1 in 3 adults with a common mental health problem are currently receiving treatment, which may include talking therapies, medication, or both.

Trends Over Time

Increase in Mental Health Issues: The number of people reporting mental health problems has risen over recent years.

Self-Harm and Suicidal Thoughts: Reports of self-harm increased by 62% between 2000 and 2014, and instances of suicidal thoughts rose by 30% in the same period.

Suicide Statistics

Total Suicides: In 2023, there were 6,069 suicides registered in England and Wales, equating to an age-standardised mortality rate of 11.4 deaths per 100,000 people, the highest rate since 1999.

Gender Disparity: Males accounted for approximately 75% of suicide deaths in 2023, with a rate of 17.4 deaths per 100,000, compared to 5.6 per 100,000 for females.

Demographic Disparities

Young Women: Over 26% of women aged 16–24 report experiencing a common mental health problem in any given week.

LGBTQ+ Youth: A 2024 survey found that 62% of LGBTQ+ young people in the UK reported experiencing symptoms of depression, and 70% reported symptoms of anxiety in the past two weeks.

Black or Black British Individuals: Approximately 23% experience a common mental health problem in any given week, compared to 17% of White British individuals.

Neurodiversity: Autism and ADHD

Autism Diagnoses: As of June 2024, there were 193,203 patients in England with an open referral for suspected autism, indicating a significant demand for diagnostic services.

ADHD Prevalence: The estimated global prevalence of ADHD is around 5% in children and 3–4% in adults in the UK.

Co-occurrence: Among individuals who are autistic but without a learning disability, 19.8% had an ADHD diagnosis in 2023–24.

Children and Young People

Prevalence: One in five children and young people in the UK are experiencing common mental health problems, with a notable rise in emergency referrals.

Economic Impact: The ongoing mental health crisis among young people is projected to result in over £1 trillion in lost lifetime earnings due to increased mental health issues affecting education and employment prospects.

Economic Costs

Scotland: The mental health crisis in Scotland is costing taxpayers £3.6 million per day, with over £1.3 billion annually spent on adult disability payments for mental and behavioural conditions.

Medication Expenditure: In 2020, the total NHS spend on medications used to treat anxiety and depression was £346.4 million, with the highest dispensing rates in the North East and North Cumbria.

Let's address the important details first to understand each mental health issue from a clinical perspective. You can skip this section and return to it later, if need be.

Clinical Insight: Understanding Mental Health

Mental health encompasses an individual's emotional, psychological, and social well-being and plays a vital role in how we think, feel, and act. It influences our ability to cope with stress, maintain relationships, make choices, and behave in various situations. Just like physical health, mental health exists on a broad spectrum; it's dynamic and can fluctuate over time due to various factors including life experiences and circumstances.

The World Health Organization (WHO) articulates mental health not merely as the absence of mental illness, but as a holistic state of well-being where individuals can:

Recognize and realize their own potential,
Effectively manage the typical stresses of daily life,
Engage in productive work that is fulfilling,
Contribute positively to their communities.

Distinguishing Mental Health from Mental Illness

It is essential to differentiate between mental health and mental illness, as they are not synonymous. One can experience poor mental health without having a diagnosed condition, just as one can hold a diagnosis of a mental illness and still experience periods of positive mental health.

Mental health involves a balance of emotions, resilience in the face of challenges, and effective emotional regulation. Conversely, mental illness refers to a range of diagnosable disorders which include, but are not limited to, depression, anxiety disorders, bipolar disorder, and post-traumatic stress disorder (PTSD). These disorders are classified in clinical manuals such as the DSM-5 (Diagnostic and Statistical Manual of Mental Disorders) or ICD-11 (International Classification of Diseases).

Similar to physical illnesses, mental illnesses are influenced by a complex interplay of biological, psychological, and social factors, such as:

Neurochemical imbalances (for example, dysregulation of neurotransmitters like serotonin or dopamine),
Genetic predispositions or vulnerabilities,
Traumatic experiences or disruptions in early attachment (such as childhood abuse or neglect),
Chronic stressors or experiences of social isolation,
Lifestyle habits that affect mental well-being, including inadequate sleep, poor nutrition, or substance use.

The Brain's Role in Mental Health

The brain is a critical component in our mental health landscape. Key regions involved include:

- The amygdala, which is responsible for emotional processing, fear responses, and detecting threats.
- The prefrontal cortex, which is essential for rational thinking, impulse control, and decision-making.
- The hippocampus, which plays a significant role in memory processing and emotional learning.

When mental health is compromised, especially in scenarios of trauma or chronic stress, the functioning of these brain systems can become dysregulated, leading to a variety of symptoms including:

- Racing thoughts or, conversely, emotional shutdown,
- Difficulty focusing or making decisions,
- Sleep disturbances, which may manifest as insomnia or excessive sleepiness,
- Mood fluctuations, panic attacks, or feelings of emotional numbness.

However, hope exists for recovery; the brain exhibits neuroplasticity, meaning that through therapeutic interventions, meaningful connections, self-awareness, and, when appropriate, medication, it can heal, rewire, and establish new patterns of thought and behaviour.

The Importance of Mental Health Awareness

Good mental health transcends merely avoiding crises; it encompasses possessing the tools and skills necessary to navigate life's highs and lows with a sense of inner stability. When we are mentally healthy, we are empowered to:

Set and sustain healthy personal boundaries,
Regulate our emotional states effectively,
Stay connected to our core values and sense of purpose,
Feel secure enough to rest, express ourselves, and cultivate loving relationships.

When mental health falters, it can permeate every aspect of life, impacting our physical health, personal relationships, professional performance, and even our sense of identity.

In our contemporary society, which often promotes relentless productivity, many individuals find themselves suffering in silence, feeling obligated to manage their struggles alone or believing that their challenges are not "serious enough."

The truth is, everyone has mental health, and just like physical health, it warrants thoughtful attention, care, and compassion. Acknowledging this reality is the first step toward nurturing a healthier, kinder world for all.

Gentle Tools for Self-Compassion

Choose one term (e.g., depression, anxiety, CPTSD) and write what *it feels like to you*. Make it personal, not clinical.

Draw or map out how your mental health feels in your body, no art skills required, just honesty.

Read one paragraph of this chapter out loud to yourself. Notice how it feels to give your experience a voice.

Reflection Prompt

What mental health label have you carried that felt heavy, inaccurate, or misunderstood? What words would you use instead?

Clinical Insight: Understanding Depression and Anxiety

Depression and anxiety are among the most prevalent mental health disorders, yet they remain widely misunderstood, even by those who experience them. While it is normal for everyone to feel low or anxious occasionally, clinical depression and anxiety represent more profound and persistent conditions that significantly disrupt an individual's thoughts, feelings, behaviours, and interactions with the world.

What Is Depression?

Depression, clinically referred to as Major Depressive Disorder (MDD), extends far beyond mere feelings of sadness. It manifests as a severe, lingering emotional state that can severely hinder a person's ability to function in daily life. Activities that were once enjoyable may lose their appeal, and even routine tasks can seem overwhelmingly burdensome.

Common symptoms of depression encompass:

- Persistent Low Mood: A continuous feeling of sadness or emptiness that does not seem to lift.
- Anhedonia: A marked loss of interest or pleasure in activities that were once enjoyable, leading to withdrawal from social interactions.
- Fatigue: Chronic fatigue or a pervasive lack of energy, making even small tasks feel daunting.
- Changes in Appetite or Weight: Significant weight loss or gain due to altered eating habits, sometimes linked to emotional states.
- Cognitive Challenges: Difficulty concentrating, making decisions, or even remembering details, which can exacerbate feelings of inadequacy.
- Sleep Disturbances: Problems with sleep, either insomnia, where falling or staying asleep becomes difficult, or hypersomnia, where excessive sleeping occurs.
- Feelings of Worthlessness: Intense feelings of guilt or hopelessness that can lead to a negative self-image and despair.

- Suicidal Thoughts: In severe instances, individuals may experience thoughts of self-harm or suicide, underscoring the critical need for intervention.

Depression arises from a complex interplay of various factors, including genetics that predispose individuals to mood disorders, neurological changes, particularly imbalances in neurotransmitters like serotonin and dopamine, adverse early life experiences, and prolonged exposure to stress. It is essential to recognize that depression is not an indicator of personal weakness or laziness; it signifies a brain and nervous system that are overwhelmed and in need of care.

What Is Anxiety?

Anxiety transitions from a natural emotional response to a clinical concern when feelings of worry, nervousness, or fear become pervasive, excessive, and debilitating. While occasional anxiety can be a rational reaction to stress, an anxiety disorder is characterized by persistent feelings of unease or dread, even in the absence of immediate threats.

Symptoms commonly associated with anxiety disorders include:

- Racing Thoughts: Constantly feeling mentally overwhelmed, often with intrusive thoughts that are difficult to control.
- Physical Tension: Muscular tightness or shaking, as the body remains in a heightened state of alert.
- Restlessness: A sense of being unable to stay calm or quiet, often accompanied by fidgeting or inability to relax.
- Sleep Issues: Difficulty in falling or staying asleep due to racing thoughts or an inability to unwind.
- Cardiovascular Symptoms: Heart palpitations, breathlessness, or other manifestations of physical stress, often mistaken for a health crisis.
- Avoidance Behaviours: Steering clear of situations that may trigger feelings of anxiety or panic, leading to increased isolation.
- Overthinking Patterns: A tendency to ruminate or excessively strategize around issues that may never occur, further enhancing anxiety levels.

In anxiety disorders, the amygdala, the part of the brain responsible for fear processing, undergoes hyperactivity, resulting in a sustained "fight-or-flight" response. This state is akin to having a fire alarm that never stops ringing, creating a false sense of danger that perpetuates feelings of urgency and distress.

When They Co-Exist

Depression and anxiety frequently co-occur, with approximately 50% of individuals diagnosed with depression also experiencing significant anxiety symptoms. In these situations, a person may feel trapped in a paradoxical state of despair and hyper-vigilance: too exhausted to engage actively with life yet too restless to find peace or respite.

- This interplay can manifest in various troubling ways:
- Cognitive Overload: For example, lying in bed with a racing mind, unable to transition from worry to rest.
- Social Withdrawal: Cancelling plans due to fear of social engagement, followed by feelings of guilt and isolation.
- Fear of Change: A yearning for different circumstances that is overshadowed by the paralyzing fear of potential consequences.

Hope Through Treatment

The encouraging reality is that both depression and anxiety are highly treatable conditions. Evidence-based treatments include:

- Psychotherapy: Approaches such as Cognitive Behavioural Therapy (CBT), Eye Movement Desensitization and Reprocessing (EMDR), or person-centred counselling, which help individuals challenge negative thought patterns and learn coping strategies.
- Pharmacotherapy: Medications, especially selective serotonin reuptake inhibitors (SSRIs), are often prescribed for moderate to severe symptoms to help stabilize mood.
- Lifestyle Modifications: Incorporating mindfulness practices, regular physical activity, maintaining good sleep hygiene, and adopting a balanced diet can significantly impact overall well-being.
- Social Support: Building and maintaining a strong social network is crucial, as emotional support from friends, family, or support groups can provide a foundation for healing.

The human brain exhibits neuroplasticity, meaning it can adapt and rewire itself over time. With compassion, consistency, and an appropriate support network, recovery from these conditions is not only possible, it is entirely within reach.

Gentle Tools for Self-Compassion

- Journal 3 moments when you survived something hard, even if no one noticed.
- Create a simple "soothe list" of things that help when your mind spirals (e.g., scent, music, blanket, walking).
- Whisper to yourself: "This isn't weakness. This is my nervous system trying to protect me."

Reflection Prompt

What does your depression or anxiety *want you to believe* about yourself? What truth could you offer back in return?

Clinical Insight: Childhood Trauma

Childhood trauma encompasses a range of distressing experiences during critical developmental phases, surpassing a child's ability to cope. These experiences can manifest as single, catastrophic events, such as a serious accident or the loss of a loved one, or as chronic, ongoing situations, such as emotional neglect, abuse, parental mental illness, or living in an unstable home environment.

What makes childhood trauma particularly potent is the brain's heightened sensitivity during these formative years. A child's nervous system and their sense of safety are still being developed. When a child faces frequent or intense emotional stress without sufficient support from caregivers or a safe environment, their brain adapts in ways that prioritize immediate survival. Unfortunately, this survival mechanism often comes at the expense of long-term emotional regulation, a healthy sense of self-worth, and trust in others and the world around them.

The ACEs Framework

The Adverse Childhood Experiences (ACEs) study is a pivotal piece of research that laid the groundwork for understanding the long-term impacts of childhood trauma. It identified ten categories of adversity that can profoundly affect a child's development:

1. Emotional, physical, or sexual abuse
2. Emotional or physical neglect
3. Witnessing domestic violence
4. Parental separation or divorce
5. Living with someone who struggles with substance misuse, mental illness, or has been incarcerated

The study's findings were compelling: as the number of ACEs a person experiences increases, so does their risk for a variety of mental health issues, addiction, chronic diseases, and even premature death. For example, individuals who report four or more ACEs are significantly more likely to encounter serious challenges like:

Depression and anxiety disorders

- Engaging in self-harming behaviours or suicide attempts
- Developing PTSD or experiencing emotional dysregulation
- Struggling with substance misuse
- Encountering poor physical health outcomes, such as heart disease or diabetes

However, it's essential to understand that trauma is not always overtly visible. It can also stem from a profound lack of nurturing, such as consistent affection, validation, and emotional safety. Children who grow up in environments where they are shamed for expressing emotions, taught to suppress their feelings, or raised by emotionally unavailable caregivers may carry invisible wounds into adulthood.

How Trauma Shapes the Brain

Experiencing repeated or intense stress during childhood can disrupt the HPA (hypothalamic-pituitary-adrenal) axis, which is critical for managing stress responses. This disruption floods the brain and body with hormones like cortisol and adrenaline, leading to a persistent state of hypervigilance (where the individual feels constantly on guard) or emotional shutdown (where they experience numbness).

The long-term neurological implications of this dysregulation can be profound, including:

- Over activation of the amygdala, the brain region responsible for fear processing and the threat response, causing heightened anxiety and fear responses.
- Underdevelopment of the prefrontal cortex, impairing areas critical for impulse control, reasoning, and decision-making.
- Atrophy of the hippocampus, affecting memory formation and emotional learning.

These neurological alterations explain why many adults who experienced childhood trauma find themselves grappling with:

Emotional flashbacks, where they relive past trauma in response to present-day situations
Challenges trusting others, often stemming from ingrained fears of betrayal

Chronic shame, leading to people-pleasing behaviours or a persistent need for external validation

Deep fears surrounding abandonment, intimacy, or vulnerability

Difficulty regulating emotions, leading to feeling overwhelmed by intense emotions or experiencing emotional numbness

Reframing Trauma: It Was Never Your Fault

It's crucial to understand that experiencing trauma is not an indicator of personal failure; rather, it reflects circumstances beyond one's control. Trauma signifies that something wrong happened to you, and your brain and body employed survival strategies, whether that be emotional avoidance, perfectionism, dissociation, or overachieving, to cope with the overwhelming situation. Your responses were not signs of weakness; they were adaptive strategies aimed at ensuring your survival during times of extreme distress.

The Good News: Healing Is Possible

Despite the deep imprints trauma can leave, the brain possesses incredible neuroplasticity, the ability to re-organize itself by forming new neural connections. This means recovery and healing from trauma are attainable. Approaches such as trauma-informed therapy, somatic therapy, Eye Movement Desensitization and Reprocessing (EMDR), inner child work, and cultivating secure relationships can all support the journey towards healing. What was once a matter of survival can transform into a journey of growth and resilience.

You can embark on the path to healing by learning to:

- Recognize your emotional triggers and patterns
- Regulate your nervous system to foster a sense of safety
- Connect with others in meaningful and secure ways
- Reclaim your narrative without feelings of shame or guilt

While your past has influenced who you are, it does not have to define your future. Healing from childhood trauma is not about erasing the pain; instead, it's about learning to carry that pain with compassion, ensuring that it no longer dictates your present or future.

Gentle Tools for Self-Compassion

23

- Write a letter to your younger self beginning with: "You didn't deserve that."
- Place one hand on your heart and say, "You were a child. You should have been safe."
- Choose one unmet childhood need (safety, affection, play) and give yourself 10 minutes to honour it today.

Reflection Prompt

What were you made to feel responsible for as a child that was never yours to carry?

Clinical insight of ADHD (Attention Deficit Hyperactivity Disorder)

Understanding ADHD: A Comprehensive Overview

Attention Deficit Hyperactivity Disorder (ADHD) is a complex neurodevelopmental condition that significantly impacts how the brain regulates attention, impulse control, and executive functioning. Despite being characterized by symptoms such as restlessness and impulsivity, ADHD is often misconstrued or trivialized as mere bad behaviour. However, it is a serious clinical condition officially acknowledged by the DSM-5, or the Diagnostic and Statistical Manual of Mental Disorders, Fifth Edition.

(The DSM-5 serves as a cornerstone for mental health professionals globally, providing a standardized approach to defining and diagnosing various mental health conditions. The criteria it establishes for ADHD are particularly detailed, allowing clinicians to differentiate between normal levels of distractibility and the kind of impairments that substantially affect daily functioning)

Symptoms and Subtypes as Defined by the DSM-5

The DSM-5 categorizes ADHD into three main presentations, each characterized by distinct symptoms:

1. Inattentive Type:
   - Easily distracted or prone to distraction, often leading to forgetfulness.
   - Difficulty sustaining attention, particularly in tasks that require prolonged concentration.
   - Frequently misplaces items essential for tasks or activities, leading to interruptions in workflow.
   - Struggles to follow through on instructions or complete tasks, which can result in unfinished projects.
   - Exhibits a "day dreamy" demeanour or appears disengaged during conversations or activities.

2. Hyperactive-Impulsive Type:
- Displays restlessness or excessive movement, often fidgeting or tapping hands or feet.
- Tends to talk excessively and may repeatedly interrupt or intrude on others' conversations.
- Engages in impulsive behaviours, making hasty decisions without adequately considering potential consequences.
- Experiences difficulty remaining still or silent, often feeling an internal drive to be in constant motion.
- Has a sensation of being "on edge" or having an unrelenting urge to act?

3. Combined Type:
Represents a blend of both inattentive and hyperactive-impulsive symptoms, making it the most common presentation of ADHD. For a formal diagnosis, the symptoms must meet specific criteria:
- They must be present for a minimum of six months.
- Symptoms should be inconsistent with the person's developmental level.
- They need to manifest across multiple settings, such as home, school, and work.
- The individual must experience functional impairment in their daily life as a result of the symptoms.

The Neurobiological Underpinnings of ADHD

ADHD is not simply a matter of poor self-control; rather, it is rooted in distinct neurobiological differences. Research utilizing brain imaging techniques has identified several key factors:
- Reduced Activity in the Prefrontal Cortex: This area of the brain is crucial for high-level cognitive functions, including planning, decision-making, focus, and impulse control. Reduced activity here can lead to challenges in managing these abilities.
- Irregular Dopamine Transmission: Dopamine is a neurotransmitter linked to motivation, reward processing, and pleasure. Abnormalities in dopamine transmission can lead to increased difficulties in regulating attention and sustained focus.
- Impaired Communication Between Brain Regions: Difficulty in the coordination of communication among various brain regions can

hinder a person's ability to switch tasks and maintain consistent attention, contributing further to challenges in daily activities.

The Consequences of Misdiagnosis or Missed Diagnosis

ADHD often presents subtly, particularly in certain populations such as women, people of colour, and those who have experienced trauma. As a result, many individuals may spend years blaming themselves for traits like forgetfulness, disorganization, or feelings of emotional overwhelm, unaware that their brains function differently.

Moreover, the overlapping symptoms of ADHD with other mental health conditions, including Generalized Anxiety Disorder, Depression, Autism Spectrum Disorder (ASD), and Complex PTSD (CPTSD) underscore the necessity for accurate diagnoses and trauma-informed assessments in clinical settings.

Pathways to Hope and Healing

The encouraging news is that ADHD is highly treatable, allowing individuals to thrive. Effective support strategies include:
Medication: This may involve stimulants (such as methylphenidate and lisdexamfetamine) or non-stimulant options, tailored to the individual's needs and response to treatment.

- Therapeutic Approaches: Cognitive Behavioural Therapy (CBT) and ADHD coaching can provide tools for managing symptoms and enhancing executive functioning.
- Lifestyle Modifications: Creating structured routines, utilizing visual reminders, employing body doubling techniques, and establishing comforting rituals can significantly improve daily functioning.
- Emphasizing Self-Compassion: Cultivating a mind-set of self-compassion can be one of the most nurturing methods for healing, helping individuals recognize their unique strengths and challenges without harsh self-judgment.

With understanding, tailored support, and effective strategies, individuals diagnosed with ADHD can not only manage their symptoms but can also harness the unique strengths that come with their neurodivergent minds, ultimately thriving in various aspects of life.

Gentle Tools for Self-Compassion

- Celebrate one thing you accomplished today, no matter how small. ADHD often hides effort behind guilt.
- Write a list titled: "Ways My Brain is Brilliant (Even if Others Don't Get It)."
- Try a "dopamine break", choose one playful, sensory-pleasing activity without guilt (music, drawing, dancing, reorganising something).

Reflection Prompt

What parts of your identity have been shaped by trying to "mask" or "keep up"? What would freedom from that look like?

Clinical Insight: Complex Post-Traumatic Stress Disorder (CPTSD)

Understanding Complex Post-Traumatic Stress Disorder (CPTSD)

Complex Post-Traumatic Stress Disorder (CPTSD) is a profound psychological condition that emerges as a consequence of enduring prolonged, repeated, or inescapable trauma, particularly during one's formative years. Unlike traditional Post-Traumatic Stress Disorder (PTSD), which typically arises from a single, acute life-threatening incident (such as an accident, assault, or natural disaster), CPTSD is rooted in chronic trauma that gradually dismantles an individual's sense of self, security, and self-worth over time.

Recognized in the ICD-11 (International Classification of Diseases), CPTSD is not yet classified as a standalone diagnosis in the DSM-5 (Diagnostic and Statistical Manual of Mental Disorders, Fifth Edition). Nonetheless, an increasing number of clinicians and trauma-informed therapists are addressing its unique presentation and complexities in their daily practice, highlighting its significance in the field of mental health.

What Causes CPTSD?

CPTSD often develops from various forms of chronic trauma, including:

- Childhood Abuse or Neglect: Experiences that can involve physical, emotional, or sexual abuse by caregivers, leading to a traumatic disruption in early attachment systems.
- Domestic Violence or Coercive Control: Ongoing exposure to intimidation, manipulation, and emotional or physical violence can create an environment of fear and helplessness.
- Human Trafficking, Captivity, or Institutional Abuse: Long-term exploitation or confinement can profoundly impact an individual's mental health.
- Long-term Emotional Abandonment or Humiliation: Repeated experiences of being devalued or neglected can distort an individual's self-perception and sense of safety.

31

- Repeated Invalidation in Early Relationships: Constantly having one's feelings or experiences dismissed can hinder emotional development and foster deep-seated self-doubt.

CPTSD is predominantly characterized by relational trauma, as the most damaging experiences frequently occur between the victim and those meant to provide safety, love, and protection. This betrayal can become internalized and profoundly affect an individual's sense of self.

Symptoms of CPTSD (as Defined by ICD-11)

CPTSD encompasses the hallmark symptoms of PTSD:

- Re-experiencing the Trauma: This may manifest as flashbacks, distressing memories, overwhelming emotions, or recurring nightmares that relive the traumatic events.
- Avoidance of Reminders: Individuals often sidestep reminders of the trauma, which can include people, places, activities, or even specific emotions tied to their experiences.
- Hyper arousal: This symptom refers to a constant state of heightened alertness which may present as being easily startled, feeling tense or on edge, and experiencing difficulty relaxing or sleeping.

In addition to these core symptoms, CPTSD introduces a significant cluster known as 'Disturbances in Self-Organisation (DSO)', which includes:

- Emotional Dysregulation: This may involve intense mood swings, episodes of anger, profound feelings of shame, or a sense of emotional numbness.
- Negative Self-Concept: Individuals may develop ingrained beliefs about themselves as unworthy, broken, or inherently unlovable, often linking their self-worth to past traumas.
- Relational Difficulties: There might be a pervasive fear of intimacy, challenges in trusting others, or a tendency to gravitate toward unhealthy relationships characterized by turmoil.

People suffering from CPTSD frequently report feelings of disconnection from their identities, an inability to form stable, trusting relationships, chronic guilt, and a pervasive sense of internalized shame that feels entwined with their sense of self.

The Brain Under Chronic Trauma

Chronic trauma can lead to significant alterations in brain structure and function:

- Amygdala Hyper activation: This area of the brain, responsible for processing emotions and threat detection, becomes overactive, keeping the individual's nervous system in a perpetual state of survival mode, manifesting as fight, flight, freeze, or fawn responses.
- Hippocampal Disruption: This impacts memory processing, resulting in some memories being vividly recalled while others remain fragmented or entirely inaccessible.
- Prefrontal Cortex Impairment: Damage to this region hinders an individual's ability to regulate emotions and respond rationally to triggers, often leading to impulsivity or emotional dysregulation.

Consequently, individuals with CPTSD may appear "emotionally intense," disengaged, or excessively sensitive, behaviours that reflect their brain's adaptation to overwhelming stressors and crises.

Why CPTSD Often Goes Misunderstood

CPTSD's roots in developmental and relational trauma can lead to a range of subtle symptoms that do not align with more dramatic PTSD presentations, sometimes obscuring the true nature of the condition. This can manifest as:
- A high-functioning adult who, despite outward success, perpetually battles anxiety and exhaustion.
- A chronic people-pleaser who suppresses their own needs to maintain a façade of safety.
- Someone who emotionally shuts down during conflict or struggles to tolerate emotional intimacy or affection.
- Persistent feelings of being "too much" and yet "not enough," leading to inner turmoil and self-doubt.

    Such presentations can result in misdiagnoses, including Borderline Personality Disorder, Bipolar Disorder, or Generalized Anxiety Disorder, while the core issue remains unresolved trauma.

Healing CPTSD: Rebuilding from the Inside Out

Recovery from CPTSD is not only possible but often a profound journey that is gradual, non-linear, and deeply relational. Healing entails:

- Regulating Your Nervous System: Developing skills to manage physiological responses to stress and trauma is crucial for recovery.
- Rebuilding a Sense of Safety: This involves fostering a secure environment both within oneself and in interpersonal relationships.
- Reclaiming Your Identity: Individuals are encouraged to disentangle their self-worth from their traumatic experiences, recognizing that they are not defined by what happened to them.

Effective therapies that support healing include:

- Trauma-informed therapy: Approaches such as Eye Movement Desensitization and Reprocessing (EMDR), Somatic Experiencing, and Internal Family Systems focus on processing trauma in a safe environment.
- Psychoeducation: Understanding the brain-body connection and the effects of trauma can empower individuals on their healing journey.
- Body-based practices: Incorporating practices like yoga, grounding techniques, and breathwork can promote physical and emotional regulation.
- Creating Safe Connections: Engaging in supportive relationships or exploring inner child work can facilitate healing through relational experiences.

CPTSD does not define you; it describes the challenges you have endured and the resilience you have demonstrated in surviving these experiences. It is a testament to your strength, and it's never too late to embark on the path toward reclaiming your sense of self and well-being. Healing is not just about getting over past trauma; it's about coming home to yourself, fostering self-compassion, and embracing your journey toward recovery.

Gentle Tools for Self-Compassion

- Place a hand on your chest and say, "I am not unsafe now, even if my body remembers differently."
- Create a grounding routine for flashback moments (e.g., cold water, scent, texture, movement).

- Draw a boundary with the past: write down what happened *then* and what's true *now*.

Reflection Prompt

What part of your past still tries to shape how safe or worthy you feel today? What would it take to gently reclaim that space?

Clinical Insight - Understanding Trauma: A Comprehensive Overview

Trauma is a complex phenomenon that extends beyond the mere occurrence of an event; it is fundamentally shaped by the impact it has on an individual. Two people may encounter the same traumatic incident but leave with vastly different emotional and psychological consequences. This disparity arises because trauma encompasses not just the events that happen to us, but also the intricate processes that unfold within us as a result of those experiences.

Defining Trauma Clinically

Clinically, trauma can be understood as the body and brain's response to overwhelming stimuli, experiences that feel threatening, inescapable, or intensely distressing. These experiences can be acute, stemming from a singular incident such as a serious accident, the loss of a loved one, or an assault. Alternatively, trauma can also manifest chronically, arising from prolonged emotional neglect, repeated abuse, or growing up in an environment that feels consistently unsafe or invalidating.

The Neuroscience of Trauma

When faced with a real or perceived threat, our brain activates a survival mechanism known as the fight, flight, freeze, or fawn response. This reaction is governed by the autonomic nervous system and involves critical brain regions:

1. Amygdala: Responsible for detecting danger and triggering fear responses.
2. Hypothalamus: Releases stress hormones like cortisol and adrenaline which prepare the body for immediate action.
3. Prefrontal Cortex: Typically helps us process information rationally, but often becomes less effective during traumatic events.

In the heat of trauma, the body is flooded with stress hormones, gearing up for protection. However, when the perceived threat lingers, or when we lack the opportunity to process the trauma properly, our nervous system can become dysregulated. This dysregulation can result in persistent and distressing symptoms, including:

- Hypervigilance: An exaggerated state of sensory sensitivity often triggered by reminders of the trauma.
- Flashbacks or Emotional Flooding: Intense reliving of the traumatic event, which can feel overwhelming.
- Avoidance: Steering clear of places, people, or activities that evoke memories of the trauma.
- Emotional Numbness or Detachment: A disconnection from one's emotions or the world around them.
- Panic Attacks or Dissociation: Sudden episodes of intense fear or a feeling of being disconnected from one's thoughts or surroundings.
- Difficulty Sleeping or Building Trust: Challenges in attaining restful sleep or forming trusting relationships.

When these symptoms persist over time, they can develop into Post-Traumatic Stress Disorder (PTSD) or Complex PTSD (CPTSD), particularly when trauma has occurred during formative years or repeatedly.

Exploring Types of Trauma

Trauma can be categorized into several distinct types, each with unique implications:

- Acute Trauma: Arises from a singular distressing event, such as a car crash, sudden death, or assault.
- Chronic Trauma: Results from enduring distress over time, such as long-term emotional abuse, bullying, or domestic violence.
- Complex Trauma: Refers to repeated and often interpersonal trauma experienced over time, typically during childhood, where escape or escape mechanisms were not accessible.
- Developmental Trauma: Occurs during pivotal stages of growth, often before the age of seven, impacting critical areas such as brain development, attachment styles, and personal identity.
- Vicarious Trauma: Involves emotional pain absorbed through the act of witnessing others' traumatic experiences, which is particularly prevalent among caregivers, therapists, and first responders.

Misconceptions About Trauma

Due to its profound effects on memory, focus, emotional regulation, and behaviour, trauma is often misdiagnosed or poorly understood. Individuals with unresolved trauma may be unfairly characterized as:

- "Too emotional"
- "Difficult" or "defensive"
- "Detached" or "cold"
- "Hyper" or "lazy"
- "Overreacting" or "too sensitive"

However, these labels often mask the true struggle of individuals who have adapted their behaviours as survival strategies in the absence of adequate support. Trauma can manifest in understated ways, such as high-functioning burnout, people-pleasing tendencies, or emotional shutdown rather than overtly dramatic symptoms.

The Hope for Healing

The remarkable news is that trauma can indeed be healed. The brain is neuroplastic, which means it has the capacity to forge new connections and pathways that promote safety and resilience. Healing doesn't imply forgetting the trauma; rather, it involves teaching the mind and body that danger has passed, permitting restoration and growth.

Healing approaches may encompass:

- Therapeutic Modalities: Techniques such as Eye Movement Desensitization and Reprocessing (EMDR), Somatic Experiencing, and Internal Family Systems therapy can be pivotal in processing trauma.
- Regulation Tools: Practices like grounding exercises, breathwork, and movement can aid in managing trauma responses.
- Relational Healing: Establishing safe, validating connections with others can nurture recovery and reinforce the sense of security.
- Self-Compassion: Embracing self-compassion allows individuals to reconnect with parts of themselves that may have been neglected or suppressed in the effort to cope.

Through these pathways to healing, individuals can reclaim their sense of safety, connection, and balance, fostering a healthier relationship with themselves and others.

Gentle Tools for Self-Compassion

- Place a hand on your chest and say, "I am not unsafe now, even if my body remembers differently."
- Create a grounding routine for flashback moments (e.g., cold water, scent, texture, movement).
- Draw a boundary with the past: write down what happened *then* and what's true *now*.

Reflection Prompt

What part of your past still tries to shape how safe or worthy you feel today? What would it take to gently reclaim that space?

Clinical Insight: Emotional Flashbacks & Nervous System Healing

When we think about "flashbacks," many envision dramatic, cinematic re-enactments of traumatic incidents. However, for numerous trauma survivors, particularly those grappling with Complex PTSD or developmental trauma, these experiences often manifest not in vivid images but in powerful, emotional waves.

An emotional flashback is characterized by a sudden and intense surge of feelings that transport you back to an earlier stage of your life, often evoking the mind-set and emotional state of a younger, more vulnerable version of yourself. Although the specific memory may elude you, your body carries the imprint of past experiences. During these episodes, one might unexpectedly encounter feelings of:

- Deep Shame: A pervasive sense of unworthiness stemming from past messages experienced in childhood or formative years.
- Worthlessness: A debilitating conviction that you don't have intrinsic value, leading to self-doubt.
- Terror and Abandonment: An intense fear of being alone or abandoned, often linked to past relational traumas.
- Rage: Anger that might feel disproportionate, drawing from unresolved feelings regarding past injustices.
- The Urge to Run, Cry, Freeze, or Shut Down: A visceral response often activated by mere reminders of distressing moments.
- Overwhelming Guilt or Self-Hate: A critical inner voice echoing sentiments of failure, sometimes unearthing feelings rooted in experiences of neglect or abuse.

These emotional flashbacks can be triggered by seemingly innocuous stimuli, a particular tone of voice, a facial expression, being overlooked, or feeling misunderstood. Despite their subtle origins, the reactions can be profound and overwhelming. This isn't a matter of being "too sensitive"; it's your nervous system orchestrating a response based on its past conditioning, essentially designed for survival.

What Happens During an Emotional Flashback?

During an emotional flashback, the body reacts as though the past traumas are occurring in real time. Research shows that trauma resides not just in our conscious thoughts but also within the body and the limbic system—especially the amygdala, which plays a crucial role in detecting threats. In such moments, your prefrontal cortex, the area responsible for reasoning and logical thinking, takes a back seat. The amygdala effectively hijacks your response, releasing stress hormones like cortisol and adrenaline that prepare the body to react.

As a result, you may find yourself:

- Going Quiet or Dissociating: Feeling detached from the present moment, almost as if you've stepped outside of yourself.
- Feeling a Sudden Urge to Flee or Self-Isolate: Responding with the instinct to escape situations that feel threatening, even if they are not.
- Struggling to Articulate What's Wrong: Finding it difficult to explain to others or even to yourself what you are experiencing emotionally.
- Feeling Like a Terrified Child in an Adult Body: Experiencing overwhelming feelings of fear or vulnerability that seem disproportionate to the current situation.

It's vital to recognize that this is not a demonstration of weakness; rather, it represents a trauma response deeply rooted in past experiences.

The Role of the Nervous System

The autonomic nervous system regulates our responses to stress and safety, comprising two main states:

1. Sympathetic (Fight or Flight): This system gears you up to confront or flee from perceived danger.
2. Parasympathetic (Rest and Digest): This state promotes relaxation and restoration, allowing the body to balance and heal.

When trauma goes unprocessed, people may find their bodies stuck in a constant state of survival. Some may endure relentless hypervigilance, continuously scanning for threats, while others might collapse into states of freeze or fawn, numbing their feelings, overly accommodating others, or feeling paralyzed.

Consequently, trauma recovery encompasses more than just altering one's thoughts; it involves instructing the body that it is safe to experience and express feelings again.

Why Nervous System Healing Matters

Nervous system healing centres on regulation rather than achieving perfection. It involves recognizing when your body has become dysregulated and learning how to comfort and restore it to a state of safety, gently, consistently, and with self-compassion.

Through the concept of neuroplasticity, the brain's ability to reorganize itself by forming new neural connections, individuals can cultivate a lasting sense of safety, even when previously their entire lives felt fraught with insecurity.

Effective healing strategies might encompass:

- Grounding Techniques: Engaging the senses through naming objects, feeling different textures, or consciously counting breaths to anchor oneself in the present.
- Somatic Practices: Incorporating movement, stretching, yoga, or shaking to release stored energy and reconnect with the body.
- Polyvagal-Informed Breath work: Focusing on extended exhalations to stimulate the vagus nerve, promoting relaxation.
- Safe Touch or Co-Regulation: Using comforting physical contact, like holding your chest, rocking, or embracing a trusted individual, to help stabilize emotional states.
- Mindful Self-Talk: Reassuring yourself with affirmations such as, "This is a body memory. I am safe now," to navigate turbulent feelings.

The core principle is to approach your responses with acceptance and kindness, rather than shame.

You're Not Broken—You're Wired for Survival

Emotional flashbacks should not be perceived as overreactions; they are echoes of wounds that were left unheard and unprocessed at the time they occurred. Now, you have the opportunity to provide yourself with what was missing back then: presence, patience, and permission to slow down.

Healing the nervous system does not equate to never facing triggers again; instead, it is about recognizing your patterns and learning how to return to a place of self-connection more swiftly and compassionately each time you find yourself in distress.

Gentle Tools for Self-Compassion

- When triggered, ask yourself: "How old do I feel right now?" Then comfort that age.
- Try the 5-4-3-2-1 technique: name 5 things you see, 4 you feel, 3 you hear, 2 you smell, 1 you taste.
- Create a "safety cue" (a word, gesture, scent) to anchor yourself when dysregulated.

Reflection Prompt

What does safety *really* feel like in your body—not just the absence of danger, but the presence of peace?

Clinical Insight: Bipolar Disorder

Bipolar disorder is a complex mood disorder characterized by significant and often unpredictable shifts in mood, energy levels, thinking patterns, and behaviour. These mood changes are much more than typical emotional highs and lows; they can be intensely disruptive, leading to challenges in personal relationships, professional environments, and overall self-esteem. Individuals with bipolar disorder may experience extreme oscillations that can feel like an emotional rollercoaster, alternating between exhilarating euphoria and debilitating despair, or profound clarity and confusion, engendering a sense of turbulence that affects their daily life.

It's important to understand that bipolar disorder is not simply a matter of being "moody" or "dramatic." It is a well-documented neurobiological condition acknowledged in the DSM-5 (Diagnostic and Statistical Manual of Mental Disorders) and impacts approximately 1 in 50 adults in the UK.

Types of Bipolar Disorder (DSM-5 Classification)

1. Bipolar I Disorder

This type is defined by the presence of at least one manic episode lasting a minimum of seven days or requiring hospitalization due to its severity. While depressive episodes often follow, they are not a mandatory criterion for diagnosis.

2. Bipolar II Disorder

This condition involves recurring patterns of hypomania, a lesser form of mania and major depressive episodes. Unlike mania, hypomania is generally less severe and rarely leads to hospitalization, but it can still significantly affect an individual's functioning.

3. Cyclothymic Disorder (Cyclothymia)

Cyclothymiacs is marked by chronic fluctuations between mild depressive symptoms and hypomanic symptoms lasting for over two years. These mood

47

swings do not meet the full criteria for either a manic or depressive episode, emphasizing the subtlety of this disorder.

What Mania and Hypomania Can Look Like?

Mania is often misunderstood. It includes not just elevated mood but also:

- Inflated self-esteem or grandiosity: Individuals may feel an exaggerated sense of self-worth or power.
- Racing thoughts and rapid speech: Conversations may become pressured, with thoughts jumping from one subject to another quickly.
- Decreased need for sleep: A person might function well on minimal sleep, mistakenly believing they have boundless energy.
- Risky behaviours: This can include impulsive spending, engaging in unprotected sexual activities, or reckless driving.
- Delusions or hallucinations: In severe instances, individuals may experience altered perceptions of reality.

Hypomania shares similar features but is less extreme; individuals may retain better control and function relatively well, although they may become overstimulated, impulsive, or irritable. This can manifest as a burst of creativity or enhanced confidence, but it may quickly turn into feelings of overwhelm or impending burnout.

What Depression Can Look Like

Depressive episodes within bipolar disorder can be profoundly debilitating and may include:

- Intense feelings of sadness, hopelessness, or emptiness: These emotions can feel overwhelming and inescapable.
- Fatigue or lack of motivation: Individuals may struggle to engage in daily activities, leading to withdrawal from social interactions.
- Feelings of worthlessness or shame: Negative self-perceptions can become pervasive, affecting self-esteem.
- Alterations in sleep and appetite: Significant changes in sleep patterns (insomnia or hypersomnia) and appetite (overeating or loss of appetite) are common.
- Suicidal thoughts or ideation: In severe cases, individuals may contemplate self-harm or suicide.

The stark contrast between the euphoric highs and the debilitating lows can be emotionally jarring. After experiencing mania or hypomania, individuals may grapple with feelings of guilt or confusion, especially if their behaviour during those phases led to negative consequences that must be addressed in their depressive state.

What Causes Bipolar Disorder?

The etiology of bipolar disorder is thought to involve a multifaceted interplay of genetic, biological, and environmental factors:

- Genetic predisposition: A family history of bipolar disorder significantly increases an individual's risk of developing the condition.
- Brain structure and function: Imaging studies have revealed structural and functional anomalies in areas of the brain that regulate mood (such as the amygdala and prefrontal cortex).
- Neurotransmitter imbalances: Abnormal levels of key neurotransmitters like dopamine, serotonin, and norepinephrine have been linked to the disorder.
- Environmental triggers: Stress, past trauma, sleep disturbances, and substance use can precipitate episodes, particularly in those with a genetic vulnerability.

What Bipolar Disorder Is Not?

It is crucial to clarify what bipolar disorder is frequently misconstrued as:

- Not simple mood swings: The severity and impact far exceed typical fluctuations in mood.
- Not a character flaw or weakness: It is a legitimate medical condition, not indicative of personal shortcomings.
- Not attention-seeking behaviour: The symptoms are deeply challenging to navigate and not performed for attention.
- Not always conspicuous: Many individuals maintain functionality and excel in professional or social settings, particularly during hypomanic episodes.

Bipolar disorder is sometimes misdiagnosed as depression, borderline personality disorder (BPD), or attention deficit hyperactivity disorder

(ADHD), especially among young individuals who may seek help predominantly during depressive phases. Therefore, precise assessment, which includes a thorough history of mood cycles, is essential.

Treatment and Hope

While bipolar disorder can be challenging to manage, it is highly treatable through a comprehensive and individualized approach:

- Mood stabilizers: Medications like lithium and lamotrigine can help regulate mood swings effectively.
- Antipsychotic medications: Useful in managing manic episodes and reducing their severity.
- Psychotherapy: Cognitive Behavioural Therapy (CBT), psychoeducation, and family-focused therapy can be key components of a treatment plan.
- Sleep hygiene and routine: Establishing a consistent sleep schedule is vital, as sleep disturbances serve as major triggers for episodes.
- Supportive relationships: Having a trusted confidant or "spotter" who can recognize early warning signs can have a transformative effect on one's ability to manage the disorder.

Many individuals with bipolar disorder can lead rich, fulfilling lives, particularly when they understand their triggers, adhere to their treatment plans, and receive support that fosters understanding rather than stigma.

You Are Not Your Diagnosis

It is important to remember that a diagnosis does not define your identity; rather, it acts as a guide, helping to illuminate the reasons behind your experiences and how best to support parts of yourself that may feel burdened. Living with bipolar disorder carries no shame; it does not render you unstable, unreliable, or unworthy of love. It is a facet of the human experience that deserves compassion, understanding, and care.

Gentle Tools for Self-Compassion

- Make a compassion list: "Here's what I needed in my highs and lows but didn't receive."

- Validate your cycles: "These are not failures, just different rhythms of my story."
- Let go of labels for one moment. What do you feel underneath the diagnosis?

Reflection Prompt

What is the difference between your true self and your symptoms and how can you start holding both with grace?

Clinical Insight: Burnout

Burnout transcends mere fatigue or the sensation of being overworked; it represents a profound state of chronic emotional, physical, and mental exhaustion that evolves from enduring stress over an extended period. This condition is often tied to the demands of our roles—whether in the workplace, caregiving, parenting, activism, or simply navigating a world saturated with high-pressure situations and trauma.

The World Health Organization (WHO) recognizes burnout as an occupational phenomenon rather than a medical diagnosis. It is characterized by three primary dimensions:

1. Emotional Exhaustion: This manifests as an overwhelming sense of depletion, where individuals feel drained of energy and unable to renew themselves, even with adequate rest or breaks. It can lead to persistent feelings of fatigue and a sense of being overwhelmed by daily responsibilities.

2. Depersonalization (or Cynicism): This involves developing a mental distance from one's work or relationships. Individuals may feel numb, irritable, or indifferent, often viewing their job or personal interactions in a detached or cynical manner. This emotional disconnect can significantly impact personal and professional relationships.

3. Reduced Personal Accomplishment: Individuals may feel ineffective or inadequate, constantly perceiving that their efforts fall short regardless of their dedication. This dimension reflects a sense of failing to meet personal or external expectations, which can exacerbate feelings of worthlessness.

How Burnout Differs from Depression

While burnout and depression may exhibit similar symptoms, they are fundamentally different. Burnout typically relates to specific roles, such as job responsibilities or caregiving duties, while depression permeates all aspects of life, affecting emotional well-being across various situations. Those experiencing burnout may find relief through rest or time away from their responsibilities, whereas individuals suffering from depression often do not experience the same reprieve.

If left unaddressed, burnout has the potential to escalate into clinical depression, particularly if individuals begin to feel a pervasive sense of helplessness, isolation, and emotional shutdown, reinforcing the importance of recognizing and addressing burnout early.

Signs & Symptoms of Burnout

Identifying burnout involves recognizing several common signs and symptoms, including:

- Chronic Fatigue and Sleep Disturbances: Persistent exhaustion that resists recovery, often accompanied by insomnia or disrupted sleep patterns.
- Increased Irritability: Heightened emotional responses, outbursts, and a general sense of numbness or disconnection from emotions.
- Cognitive Difficulties: Challenges with concentration, memory retention, and decision-making, leading to decreased productivity and increased frustration.
- Social Withdrawal: Isolating oneself from friends, family, and responsibilities, often as a coping mechanism or defence against further stress.
- Emotional Detachment: A fading connection to work, loved ones, or activities that were once fulfilling, leading to a diminished sense of joy and purpose.
- Feelings of Inadequacy: The persistent belief that no matter the effort expended, it will never be enough, fostering a continuous cycle of self-doubt.
- Physical Ailments: An increase in stress-related symptoms such as headaches, gastrointestinal issues, or tension-related pain.
- Maladaptive Coping: Relying on substances, food, or excessive screen time to manage overwhelming feelings, which can further entrench the cycle of burnout.

The Role of the Nervous System in Burnout

It's crucial to understand that burnout is not merely a psychological issue; it encompasses physiological aspects as well. Prolonged stress activates the hypothalamic-pituitary-adrenal (HPA) axis, which can flood the body with cortisol and other stress hormones. Over time, excessive cortisol levels can dysregulate the nervous system, pushing individuals into a constant state of fight, flight, freeze, or fawn, a state that inhibits the body's ability to respond to stressors or engage in self-care effectively.

To illustrate, burnout can be likened to leaving a light switch on for too long, eventually, the system becomes drained, unable to function normally or to recuperate.

Why We Ignore the Signs

For many, the initial signs of burnout go unnoticed or unrecognized. Instead of addressing their feelings, individuals often push themselves harder, internalizing their exhaustion as a lack of discipline, laziness, or personal failure. Cultural messages that glorify hustle and relentless productivity can further complicate matters, making the act of slowing down feel like an immoral shortcoming or a sign of weakness.

This pattern can be particularly pronounced in trauma survivors or perfectionists, where self-worth becomes inextricably linked to performance. In these cases, rest may be perceived as a failure or an unsafe indulgence, reinforcing the cycle of burnout.

Burnout Recovery Begins with Permission

Recovery from burnout hinges on granting oneself permission, permission to take necessary steps toward healing and self-care, including:

- Permission to Slow Down: Allow yourself to take breaks, even when tasks feel urgent or pressing.
- Permission to Rest: Recognize that rest is not a reward for productivity; it is a fundamental aspect of well-being.
- Permission to Disappoint Others: Understand that prioritizing your mental health may lead to disappointing others, but this is essential for your preservation.
- Permission to Re-evaluate: Take the time to reconsider not just your daily schedule but also your self-worth, acknowledging that you are more than your output.

Burnout recovery is not merely about minimizing activities; it is a deep reconnection with your intrinsic needs, bodily sensations, and personal boundaries. It involves fostering a healthier relationship with yourself, one that values rest and self-compassion as integral components of a fulfilled life.

Gentle Prompt for Reflection:

Take a quiet moment and ask yourself, without judgment:

"What am I still carrying that was never meant to be mine?"
The pressure to always be available?
The belief that rest must be earned?
The fear that slowing down means failure?

Now gently consider:

What would it look like to give yourself permission today, just one small permission, that honours your humanity, not your productivity?

Write it down.
It doesn't have to be big.
It just has to be *honest*.

Clinical Insight- Substance Misuse & Trauma – The Temporary Escape That Becomes a Trap

When the Bottle Numbs What Words Cannot

Substance misuse and trauma often intertwine, not by mere coincidence, but because of a deep-seated, unmet need. For many trauma survivors, the initial foray into substance use isn't rooted in recklessness, but rather in a desperate search for relief. This pursuit often starts as a beacon of hope, a way to escape the unbearable weight of memories, emotions, and experiences that feel insurmountable.

For many, drugs, alcohol, food, gambling, or even compulsive scrolling on social media are not merely pursuits of pleasure or thrill. Instead, they are coping mechanisms, attempts to numb the pain and suffering that seem inescapable. Trauma often simmers beneath the surface, manifesting in various forms such as shame, intrusive flashbacks, hypervigilance, or a profound sense of chronic emptiness. In these moments, when the mind becomes unbearable, the body instinctively reaches for anything that offers a semblance of silence and peace.

This behaviour is not indicative of weakness; it speaks to a fundamental alteration in an individual's wiring due to trauma. When trauma engenders a nervous system that's perpetually on high alert, moments of stillness can become immensely daunting. Thus, substance use evolves into a method for "slowing the noise," quieting persistent flashbacks, or numbing grief that feels too painful to articulate. What begins as a coping mechanism for immediate relief can spiral into a debilitating cycle of dependency, compounding feelings of pain, shame, and a profound sense of self-alienation.

Why Trauma Survivors Are Vulnerable to Addiction

Trauma has a profound impact on the brain, leading to significant dysregulation in the brain's reward and stress systems. This dysregulation can affect individuals in several key ways:

- The amygdala, the brain's fear centre, becomes hyperactive, leading to increased feelings of fear, anxiety, and reactivity.
- The prefrontal cortex, responsible for rational thought, decision-making, and impulse control may become underactive, impairing one's ability to make sound decisions.
- The dopamine system, which governs pleasure and motivation, can become blunted due to prolonged exposure to trauma or chronic stress, making it difficult to find joy in everyday life.
- The hypothalamic-pituitary-adrenal (HPA) axis, which controls the body's response to stress, can become overactive, flooding the system with stress hormones like cortisol and adrenaline. This results in chronic overstimulation and heightened anxiety.

Substances can temporarily hijack these dysregulated systems, creating a false sense of balance: dopamine levels rise, fear diminishes, and intrusive thoughts blur. However, this artificial regulation can ultimately harm the brain's natural equilibrium, exacerbating dysregulation once sobriety is attempted.

Moreover, substances can mask emotional pain and unprocessed memories. The glass of wine before bed, which supposedly aids in sleep, may truly be muting panic attacks disguised as insomnia. The joint consumed before social interactions may momentarily ease the sting of old wounds from rejection. Compulsive eating may serve as a salve for an abandoned inner child yearning for safety and comfort.

The Cycle of Relief → Guilt → Shame → Use

This heart-breaking spiral encapsulates the experience of many trauma survivors:

1. Pain Resurfaces: Often triggered by stress, memories, or emotional flashbacks, this pain can feel overwhelming and inescapable.
2. Substance Use: In a bid to soothe this pain, individuals turn to substances for temporary relief, seeking an escape from their emotional turmoil.

3. Guilt and Shame: Following substance use, feelings of guilt and shame often emerge. Thoughts like, "Why do I do this to myself?" or "I should be stronger" become pervasive.
4. Isolation: The shame fuels a sense of isolation, reinforcing negative beliefs: "I'm broken," "I'm too much," or "I deserve this."
5. Repetition: This cycle continues, not out of desire but driven by an innate urge for survival.

Substance misuse emerges not from a quest for pleasure but rather as a strategy for pain management.

Addiction as a Survival Strategy

It's crucial to acknowledge that many individuals grappling with substance misuse are remarkably strong. They have faced challenges and endured traumas that most cannot fathom, often continuing to push forward not with healthy coping mechanisms but with whatever means they could access. In this context, substances become more than a failure; they transform into a resource, an imperfect solution to the overwhelming suffering they face.

Understanding the reasons behind this behaviour doesn't excuse harm or deny consequences; rather, it illuminates the "why," allowing for a more compassionate lens through which to view their struggles. Lasting recovery demands more than mere willpower; it necessitates healing the wounds that rendered escapism necessary in the first place.

The Path to Recovery

Recovery from trauma-related substance misuse is rarely a straightforward journey. It involves compassion, support, and often professional assistance. Recovery is not about deprivation; it's about reclaiming connection, safety, and self-trust. A trauma-informed recovery approach may include:

- Therapeutic modalities like Eye Movement Desensitization and Reprocessing (EMDR), somatic experiencing, or trauma-focused cognitive behavioural therapy (CBT).
- Participating in 12-step programs or alternative recovery options like SMART Recovery.
- Engaging in practices aimed at regulating the nervous system to help manage cravings and emotional flashbacks.

- Finding community support in safe spaces where one's story can be shared without judgment.

Gentle Truths

- You are not defined merely as "an addict." You are a person who adapted to pain in the best way you knew how, given your circumstances.
- Sobriety is not a punishment; it's about reclaiming your presence, your peace, and your inherent power.
- Healing does not necessitate perfection. Setbacks don't erase progress. Each moment of awareness is a victory that deserves recognition.

Gentle Tools for Self-Compassion

1. Harm Reduction Journal: Write without judgment about your substance use. Ask yourself: What am I using? Why do I think I need it right now? What feelings am I attempting to avoid or soothe? This practice builds awareness without inviting shame.

2. Crisis Box: Create a "Crisis Box" filled with grounding tools, scented oils, journals, affirmations, calming playlists, photographs, textured items that you can reach for during moments of craving.

3. Practice Name & Nurture: When cravings arise, pause and reflect: "What do I need right now that this substance is attempting to give me?" Then offer yourself a small act of nurture in place of the substance.

Gentle Tools for Self-Compassion

- **Harm Reduction Journal:** Without judgement, write: *What am I using? Why do I think I need it right now? What feeling am I trying to avoid or soothe?* This builds awareness without shame.
- **Create a "Crisis Box"** filled with grounding tools (scented oils, a journal, affirmations, a calming playlist, photos, textures). Reach for this when urges arise.
- **Practice Name & Nurture:** When you feel a craving, pause and ask: *"What do I need right now that this substance is trying to give me?"* Then offer a small act of nurture in its place.

Reflection Prompt

What pain or memory does your substance use try to silence?
What would it feel like to meet that pain with kindness instead of avoidance?

Living with It — My Reality of Mental Health

I used to harbour the unsettling belief that there was something inherently wrong with me. It wasn't the dramatic narrative you often see in films, filled with tearful breakdowns and intense emotional confrontations. No, the struggle was much subtler an insidious feeling of disconnection that lingered beneath the surface, both from myself and from the world around me.

On some days, I would walk through life feeling utterly numb, as if I were drifting through a vast ocean without being touched by its waves. Each moment felt distant, as if I were a mere observer rather than an active participant. Conversely, other days would engulf me in a tide of overwhelming sensations, the cacophony of life felt like a relentless storm, each sound and feeling pressing down on me like a heavy weight. Mornings were particularly brutal; I would awaken feeling engulfed by fatigue, often needing to rally every ounce of willpower just to rise from bed. I would plaster on a smile during conversations, dutifully nodding along while my mind danced off to faraway places, far removed from the here and now. Yet, when silence finally enveloped me, I would implode, retreating into a self-imposed shell, longing for solace but feeling lost in my own thoughts.

For an extended period, I convinced myself that this experience was merely a routine aspect of life. However, as time unfolded, I came to a different realization, it was not just a quirky trait of my character but rather a manifestation of something deeper and more pervasive. While my struggles were unique to me, I discovered that numerous others carried similar burdens.

Everyone's Talking About It, But...

Mental health has increasingly become a focal point of conversation, showcasing itself in everything from marketing campaigns to trending social media hashtags, and even in corporate training sessions on well-being. "It's okay not to be okay," the phrases echo around us, yet no one dives deeper to clarify the intricate tapestry of what "not okay" truly entails.

To me, "not okay" feels like being ensnared within a completely transparent box; I can peer out and witness life unfolding vividly around me, hear the laughter and joy of others, yet it all seems to occur a step removed from my reality. It creates an unsettling dichotomy where I am both present and absent at once, like watching a captivating movie without having any control over its narrative.

Some moments are consumed by a relentless undercurrent of anxiety, where my thoughts volley uncontrollably through an endless array of imagined scenarios, each one more daunting than the last, racing against time as I struggle to catch my breath. On other days, the spectre of depression looms large, dragging me down with invisible weights; even the most mundane activities, such as smiling at a passing stranger or initiating a conversation, transform into Herculean challenges.

I am neither lazy nor antisocial; I am persistently putting forth effort in a silent battle.

What I Wish People Knew

Mental health extends far beyond mere diagnostic labels; it is the lens through which we interpret and narrate the nuances of our life experiences. Some days, the fog lifts, and my thoughts feel clear and cohesive, while on other days, even the simplest task can seem monumental, cloaked in a fog that obscures my ability to function. My emotional landscape can shift drastically; I can find myself trapped in a spiral of over-analysis or experience a complete emotional blackout without warning. I have shed tears alone in office bathrooms, yet managed to laugh and engage at social gatherings, masking the turmoil brewing beneath the surface. We become adept at wearing a mask, particularly when the fear of being a burden looms large, preventing us from sharing our internal struggles.

But the harsh truth is that concealing our feelings offers no solace; it merely inflicts another layer of pain.

The Statistics Are Real—So Am I

I stumbled upon a stat stating that 1 in 4 individuals experiences mental health issues annually. I suppose I belong to that statistic and perhaps you do as well.

It's sobering to acknowledge how many of us don a façade of bravery, pretending everything is alright when, in reality, we are just persevering, not out of a sense of strength, but because we feel we lack the permission to be vulnerable and fall apart.

Initially, I hesitated to voice my challenges, fearing judgment or, even more distressing, dismissal. I would often hear statements like, "You don't seem depressed," or "You have nothing to complain about." But mental health doesn't conform to anyone's predefined notions of what it should look like.

What Helped Me Start Healing?

One of the most difficult truths I confronted was this: No one can rescue you from your own struggles. Recognizing this reality felt burdensome at first, but gradually, I came to realize that the source of my healing didn't reside in grand gestures but in small, intentional daily practices.

I sought a therapist who genuinely listened, providing me with a safe haven where I could freely explore my thoughts and emotions without judgment. I turned to journaling, pouring my inner turmoil onto the page until I began to unravel the chaotic whirlwind inside me. I learned to verbalize what I felt instead of opting for numbness, a practice that was both liberating and terrifying. I made a conscious decision to open up to someone in my life, despite my instinct to push people away and shut down entirely.

In this process, I learned that enduring this struggle was not an indication of weakness; rather, it was an emblem of my strength and resilience. I came to realize that healing wasn't about reverting to the person I once was; it was about evolving into the individual I was meant to be, embracing a new understanding of myself along the way.

If You're Reading This...

If any part of this resonates with you, I implore you to grasp this critical truth: you are not alone. Whether you find yourself curled up in bed, scrolling through your phone in search of connection, or sandwiched among strangers on a bustling train, feeling utterly invisible, understand that many people are carrying the same burdens that you are.

This book does not offer a magical solution; it serves instead as a space, a conversation an oasis for unpacking the emotions and thoughts we've been conditioned to keep bottled up inside.

You are not crazy, nor are you broken. You are human. And your mental well-being deserves the same attention, care, and compassion that we extend to others.

Personal Reflection: My Smile Was My Shield

For a long time, I believed that I had no justification for feeling overwhelmed or distressed. I had a stable job, a secure roof over my head, and a circle of people who cared for me deeply. Yet, despite these blessings, waves of guilt often washed over me, convincing me that my emotional struggles were insignificant in comparison to others. I didn't realize that emotional pain is not a competition; it doesn't require a hierarchy. Instead, it simply demands acknowledgment and understanding.

In my quest to be a reliable friend and support for those around me, I often neglected my own well-being. I feared being perceived as needy or fragile, so I plastered a smile on my face and became the go-to person for others in times of need. I offered my support and my listening ear, all the while hiding my own turmoil behind closed doors. The disconnect between my public persona and private reality grew wider, and eventually, I found myself unravelling.

The turning point came when I finally allowed myself to admit that I wasn't okay, even if it was just to myself. That simple act of honesty opened the door to healing and self-acceptance. It was the moment I learned that acknowledging my struggles was not a sign of weakness, but a vital step toward recovery.

Practical Tools for Gentle Self-Compassion

1. The 5% Rule – On particularly difficult days, release the pressure of aiming for perfection. Instead of striving for 100%, focus on achieving just 5%. Small steps matter, whether it's brushing your teeth, opening a window to let in fresh air, or even replying to a single text message. Remember, every bit of progress counts, no matter how minor it may seem.

2. Mindful Pause Practice – Carve out 2 minutes in your day, away from distractions. Set a timer, sit in silence, and ask yourself: "What's happening inside me right now?" Allow your breath to flow naturally as you simply observe your thoughts and feelings without the urge to fix or judge them. This practice nurtures self-awareness, helping you connect with your inner self.

3. Support Circle Audit – Reflect on the key relationships in your life by writing down three names. Identify one person who genuinely listens, another who brightens your day with laughter, and a third who consistently shows up for you. When you find yourself in a tough spot, reach out to just one of these individuals. Their support can provide the encouragement you need during challenging times.

Reflection Prompt: Embrace This Moment of Self-Care

Take a moment to pause—breathe deeply. It's easy to get caught up in what society tells us mental health should look like. But right now, focus on what mental health truly means to you, in this very moment.

Don't worry about finding the perfect words; just express your truth as it is. This space is yours alone.

Now, let's delve a little deeper…

If your heart could speak, what would it say to you today? Would it long for a moment of rest, perhaps some reassurance, or just a quiet moment of peace? How would you respond to it?

Allow this to be a gentle conversation between you and that part of yourself that has always been there, patiently waiting to be acknowledged.

There's no need to fix anything right now, just take a moment to listen and write down whatever comes to mind. Your feelings are valid, and this is a safe space for you.

I want you to know that I'm here with you. Please take a break if you need it, and come back when you're ready.

When the Mind Becomes Heavy – Living with Depression and Anxiety

Some days, I feel everything, every raw emotion flooding through me like a powerful tide. Other days, I feel nothing at all, wrapped in a heavy fog of indifference that dulls every sensation. It's strange, really, how I can share laughter in a group chat while feeling completely empty inside, as if I'm merely playing a role. I can navigate an entire day with barely a clue about what I actually felt, it's bewildering. Even worse is the nagging feeling of knowing that I might be avoiding something significant.

This isn't just a momentary bad mood. This is depression, a shadow that lingers and weighs heavily. This is anxiety, a constant hum of unease that never quite fades. This is what it's like when your own mind becomes a battlefield, a place of conflict between despair and hope.

What Depression Feels Like (For Me).

It's not always marked by tears or heartache; sometimes, it's just silence, a silence that wraps around me like a thick blanket. I find myself staring blankly, trapped in my own thoughts, feeling empty in response to things I once cherished. For me, depression manifests in several ways:

- I sit in the shower for too long, not because I enjoy the warmth of the water, but because I can't muster the courage to face the day that lies ahead.
- I scroll through messages on my phone, feeling the weight of each response, devoid of the energy needed to engage.
- I question myself incessantly, wondering if I'm just lazy, broken, or somehow both, hopelessly entangled in my own doubts.
- I either sleep excessively, trying to escape reality, or I lay awake staring at the ceiling, unable to close my eyes even for a moment.
- Guilt clings to me for doing nothing, while shame floods my thoughts when I manage to accomplish even the smallest task.

People often advise, "Just go for a walk," but they fail to understand that even the simple act of brushing my teeth sometimes feels like climbing Everest, an insurmountable challenge.

I want to feel better. I genuinely do, but under the crushing weight of it all, I often lose sight of who I am, the essence of me buried beneath layers of despair.

What Anxiety Feels Like (For Me).

Anxiety manifests as noise, a cacophony of intrusive thoughts that never seems to let up. My mind spirals into a whirlwind over scenarios that haven't even happened yet, constructing mountains out of molehills. I find myself sweating during phone calls, rehearsing my responses in my head, only to later berate myself for how I delivered them.

Anxiety looks like:

- Racing thoughts that invade my mind while I try desperately to find solace in sleep.
- A tightness in my chest that grips me in public spaces, making me feel trapped in a bubble surrounded by people, yet profoundly alone.
- Cancelling plans that I genuinely wished to keep, torn between the desire for connection and the paralyzing fear of social interactions.
- A stomach perpetually bracing for impact, as if anticipating an impending crisis.
- Overthinking every conversation, I've had that day, often dredging up memories from years past, unable to escape the cycle of self-doubt.

Anxiety creates this yearning to be seen while simultaneously inducing a paralyzing fear of being noticed. It's the constant second-guessing of every decision, the feeling of being caught in a fight-or-flight mode when there's actually no danger present. It's simply exhausting.

When They Both Show Up.

When depression and anxiety team up, it's a brutal clash. Depression whispers, "Why bother?" while anxiety counters with, "What if you mess it up?" They clash in my mind, leaving me trapped in a state of paralysis, oscillating between overthinking and an overwhelming urge to give up.

At times, I can't breathe. At other moments, I can't summon the energy to care. Sometimes, I struggle to even articulate my feelings because they seem so chaotic and incomprehensible, not just to others, but even to myself. When someone asks, "What's wrong?" I simply respond with, "I'm tired." It feels like the simplest answer, yet it barely scratches the surface of the storm within.

What Helped Me (Eventually).

It wasn't a quick fix or a miracle cure. The process was slow, clumsy, and often uncomfortable, but it marked the beginning of a long journey toward healing.

- I started journaling, pouring out the thoughts I was too scared to voice aloud, letting the words unfurl onto the page.
- I learned to name the thoughts that haunted me instead of allowing them to consume my every waking moment.
- I began to let people in, even when my instinct was to retreat into solitude, realizing that connection could be a lifeline.
- I knew that self-care isn't selfish; resting doesn't equate to laziness.
- I came to terms with the notion that seeking help isn't a flaw, it's a deeply human thing to do.

Therapy offered me tools and insights I never anticipated, and, eventually, medication became a part of my path. But perhaps most importantly, I learned that I wasn't alone. I discovered there were others out there—trying, hurting, and healing, all in their own ways.

If You're in This Right Now...

I want you to remember this: you are not a burden. You are not weak for feeling this way. You are allowed to struggle while still being deserving of love, peace, and joy. Even if today all you managed to do was get out of bed, that counts. Even if you merely made it to the next hour, that matters.

Personal Reflection: My Smile Was My Shield

73

For a long time, I believed I had no right to feel overwhelmed or emotionally worn down. On the surface, my life appeared stable: I had a secure job that paid the bills, a safe place to lay my head at night, and a circle of friends and family who genuinely cared about my well-being. By conventional measures, my life looked "fine." Yet, beneath that seemingly calm exterior, I found myself drowning in a tidal wave of guilt, constantly fixating on the struggles of others. I compared my pain to theirs, convincing myself that my feelings were inconsequential, unworthy of attention or validation. I had ingrained in my psyche the notion that emotional suffering needed justification, that it must be anchored by trauma or tragedy to be valid. But as I've come to realize, pain isn't measured on a hierarchy. It simply requires acknowledgment.

In my relentless pursuit to be the dependable one, the friend who always shows up, the one who maintains a façade of togetherness, I lost sight of myself. I donned my smile like a protective mask, taking on the roles of the listener, the fixer, and the helper. But the irony is that when the chaos of the day subsided, and the world fell silent, I crumbled. The chasm between the person I projected to the world and the turmoil I felt inside grew wider, until I finally reached a breaking point.

The pivotal moment I experienced was not marked by a dramatic breakdown but rather by an embrace of quiet honesty. I took a deep breath and admitted to myself first that I wasn't okay. That humble realization opened the floodgates to healing. While it didn't magically resolve all my issues overnight, it granted me the courage to remove my mask. It encouraged me to be authentic, to stop fleeing from my true self and my feelings.

Recognizing that I was struggling didn't render me weak; it conferred a surprising liberation. That moment became my first taste of self-acceptance, and I've been learning how to breathe into that acceptance ever since.

Practical Tools for Gentle Self-Compassion

1. The 5% Rule: When the weight of the world feels unmanageable, strive for just 5%. This isn't about striving for perfection or tackling everything at once. Instead, focus on one small act: drinking a glass of water, changing your shirt, or responding to one message. Progress doesn't always need to be loud and triumphant; sometimes, it whispers softly, inviting you to take small steps.

2. Mindful Pause Practice: Dedicate just 2 minutes to being quiet. Put away your phone and eliminate distractions. Sit comfortably and tune in to your breath. Ask yourself, "What's happening inside me right now?" Be receptive to the answers that flow forth without judgment. You don't need to rush to fix anything; simply acknowledging your feelings can be a profound act of self-love.

3. Support Circle Audit: Take a moment to jot down three names:
- One person who listens to you without passing judgment.
- One person who never fails to make you laugh.
- One person who shows up for you, no matter what.

This week, reach out to one of those individuals. You don't need to delve into heavy conversations, merely allowing for connection can be healing in itself.

Prompt: If your heart could send you a message today, what would it say?

Write back to it, allowing your thoughts to flow freely, unfiltered and raw. Your heart might be yearning for rest, seeking forgiveness, desiring softness, or requesting strength. Whatever it communicates to you, take the time to listen deeply. Respond with compassion and kindness, honouring the message it carries.

Personal Reflection: Practical Tools for Gentle Self-Compassion

Navigating the depths of depression or the chaotic whirlwind of anxiety can feel like an insurmountable challenge. In these moments, even the smallest acts of self-care can seem like mountains to climb. Yet, healing doesn't always manifest as grand transformations or sweeping changes. Sometimes, it resides in those delicate, fleeting moments of grace we extend to ourselves, subtle victories that whisper, "You're still here. You're still trying."

If you take away only one message from this chapter, let it be this: You don't have to achieve perfection or do it all at once. What you truly need is to begin exactly where you are.

Consider choosing one of the following tools, not as a rigid demand, but as a gentle invitation to nurture yourself:

The 5% Rule

When the weight of everything feels crushing, release the pressure to reach that elusive 100%. Instead, ask yourself: What does 5% effort look like for me today? Maybe it's as simple as sipping a glass of water, opening a window to let in fresh air, or sending a quick text to a friend. Embrace this small effort and recognize it for what it is: enough. Remember, progress isn't only about scale; it's about your personal journey.

Mindful Pause Practice

Dedicate just two minutes to breathe intentionally. In this brief respite, focus solely on your breath without the urge to fix anything or pass judgment on your feelings. Instead, ask yourself, "What am I feeling right now?" Allow whatever arises to simply be. This awareness, however uncomfortable, is an important part of healing; it's the moment where understanding starts to unfold.

Support Circle Audit

Take a moment to write down the names of three individuals who play significant roles in your life:
1. Someone who truly listens and provides a safe space for your thoughts.
2. Someone who brings joy and laughter, helping lighten your burdens.
3. Someone who consistently shows up for you, no matter the circumstances.
Now, reach out to just one of these individuals. You don't need to say much, just let them know you're thinking of them or that you could use their support. Opening up to someone else can be one of the bravest forms of self-care.

Reflection Prompt: Embrace This Moment of Self-Care

If you could give your depression or anxiety a voice, what would it say? And more importantly, what would you say back? Take a moment to connect with those voices; understanding them may be the first step on your journey toward healing.

Find a quiet space where you feel comfortable, if only for a few moments. Let this time be entirely dedicated to you. If your heart could speak freely right now, what would it say? Would it urge you to slow down and breathe more deeply? Would it voice a need for forgiveness, for yourself or others?

Would it remind you of your inherent worth, no matter what challenges you've faced?

Now, take pen to paper. Write back to your heart. Allow the page to hold your thoughts, letting them flow out freely, without concern for messiness, honesty, or filtering. There's no judgment here, only the truth of your feelings.

You've been carrying so much for so long. Remember, you are still here. That alone is something to honour and celebrate. Every small step matters, and every moment of self-compassion contributes to your journey of healing.

Finding Strength in the Storm – Building Emotional Resilience

Before we move onto this chapter, check-in with yourself, take a deep breath and a pause.

I used to believe that resilience was synonymous with toughness, that it meant I had to bottleneck my emotions, never cry, and never ask for assistance. I was convinced that if I ever fell apart, it would signal a personal failure. However, I finally woke up to the truth: resilience is not about being unbreakable; rather, it's about gathering the strength to piece yourself back together time and time again, even when you're weary and the weight of it all feels unbearable.

I Didn't Think I Was Strong

For a significant part of my life, I didn't feel strong at all. In fact, I felt incredibly fragile. Exhaustion clung to me like a shadow, and I was constantly on edge, as if one slight inconvenience could send me spiralling into chaos. Despite this, I pressed on, often without understanding the motivation behind my persistence. It was in the midst of this turmoil that I began to grasp that true resilience doesn't involve masking my struggles or pretending that everything is alright.

It means allowing myself to truly feel, acknowledging my emotions and choosing to move forward, regardless of how difficult that may be. It means confessing my struggles without allowing them to define my worth. It involves actively learning to soothe my own pain rather than burying it deep inside. This, I realized, is the definition of real strength.

How I Started Rebuilding Myself

The journey to rebuild my spirit was not instantaneous; there was no dramatic revelation that sparked change. Instead, it was a series of subtle, yet profound, choices made during the darkest of times. I began to pay attention to my innermost self, the real me hidden beneath layers of fear, shame, and emotional numbness. The following practices became critical to my healing:

79

1. Naming My Emotions

In the past, my emotional vocabulary was limited; responses like "I'm fine" or "I'm tired" masked my deeper feelings of anxiety, loneliness, and grief. Once I learned to articulate my emotions accurately, a transformative shift occurred. I began asking myself reflective questions: What am I really feeling in this moment? Where do those feelings reside in my body? What events triggered these sensations? By labelling my emotions, I regained a sense of control over them, as if I was no longer drowning but instead learning to navigate the waters.

Learning to Soothe Myself

There were countless nights when I found myself seated on the floor, overwhelmed and trembling. Back then, I believed I needed someone else to rescue me. Today, I know how to be my own support system. Practical techniques that have helped me include:

- Practicing a calming breath technique—breathing in for a count of four, holding for four, exhaling for four, and holding again for four to create a rhythm of calm.
- Speaking to myself the way I would comfort a dear friend, reminding myself that I am worthy of compassion.
- Placing my hand on my chest and reassuring myself with words like, "You're safe now."
- Connecting with nature by walking barefoot on grass or using something cold to ground myself emotionally.
- Allowing tears to flow without shame, recognizing that crying can be a release rather than a sign of weakness.

Although I still have moments of vulnerability, I now possess the tools to uplift myself.

Letting People In

This step proved to be the most challenging for me. I had long believed that asking for help was a sign of weakness, yet the burden of carrying my struggles alone nearly broke me. One fateful day, I mustered the courage to open up to a trusted friend. I didn't share my entire story, just enough to convey my pain. To my surprise, they didn't flee or cast judgment; they simply listened. That simple act of validation transformed everything. It was a powerful reminder that I need not navigate my challenges in isolation.

Challenging My Inner Critic

For years, my internal dialogue was harsh, echoing messages like: "You're too much," "You're not trying hard enough," and "No one genuinely cares." I allowed that voice to dictate my thoughts. Now, I actively challenge those negative beliefs. I ask myself: Is this thought based on reality or merely driven by fear? Would I voice such criticism to a friend? Is there an alternative perspective I could consider? Gradually, I'm learning to communicate with myself in a way that embodies the kindness I naturally extend to others. Though uncomfortable, this process is healing.

Remembering Why I Keep Going

Even on days when I feel particularly low, I remind myself that there's still so much left to experience and discover. I reflect on:
- Who I aspire to become
- The sense of peace that remains elusive, yet possible
- The wonderful people I have yet to meet
- The version of myself that is gradually coming into being

This perspective fosters resilience, maintaining hope even when times feel overwhelmingly bleak.

If You Grew Up in Chaos…

If your childhood was marred by stress, silence, or an urgent need for survival, the concept of resilience may feel unfamiliar. You probably had to mature before your time, developing strength by necessity rather than choice. As an adult, you might be in the process of unlearning the belief that love must be earned and that pain needs to be concealed. Later in this book, we will explore the ABC Model, a straightforward yet powerful tool that helped me understand how my past wounds influence my present reactions. But for now, it's crucial to recognize this:
- You have the right to rest.
- You have the right to feel.
- You have the right to heal at your own pace.

81

Additional Insight: The Science of Resilience

Resilience isn't about being unaffected by adversity, it's about adapting, bending without breaking, and finding ways to recover. According to psychological research, resilience involves cognitive flexibility, emotional regulation, and strong social connections. It's not a trait you're born with; it's a skill you build over time.

The brain's neuroplasticity means we can actually rewire our thinking through practices like mindfulness, positive self-talk, and therapy. By understanding our triggers and self-soothing techniques, we become less reactive and more responsive, creating emotional safety within ourselves.

Personal Reflection: The Day I Didn't Fall Apart

I remember a day when everything went wrong, bad news, a panic spiral, and an argument that left me shaken. In the past, that would have unravelled me completely. But instead of shutting down, I paused, breathed deeply, and gave myself space to process.

I didn't pretend I was okay. I just didn't abandon myself. That was resilience, not because I was "strong," but because I chose to stay with myself in the pain. That was new for me.

Practical Tools to Build Resilience

1. Anchor Phrase" Practice – Create a calming statement to repeat in hard moments: "This will pass." "I've survived worse." "I can do hard things." Repetition rewires belief.

2. Emotion Wheel Check-In – Use an emotion wheel (available online) to name your specific emotion. Going beyond "sad" or "angry" helps build emotional clarity.

3. Post-Stress Ritual – After a stressful event, do something kind for your body: drink warm tea, stretch, journal. This teaches your nervous system what safety feels like again.

Prompt: Think of a moment that tested your limits. How did you survive it? What strength did that moment reveal that you didn't realise you had?

Personal Reflection: Gentle Self-Compassion Tools

Building emotional resilience isn't about being impervious to life's challenges; it's about bending when needed, finding softness amidst sharp moments. It's about choosing to stay present, even when all you want to do is retreat. Here are some practices that I hold close, not because I've mastered them, but because they resonate with where I am in my journey.

Name It to Tame It:

When the wave of overwhelm crashes over you, pause for a moment and ask, "What am I truly feeling?" Take a moment to name that emotion and allow it to be there without any judgment. It's okay to feel.

Create a Soothing Ritual:

Try this simple breathing exercise: inhale for 4 counts, hold for 4, exhale for 4, hold for 4, and then repeat. You can place a hand on your chest as you do this and speak kindly to yourself. These small acts can help calm a turbulent mind and bring a little peace.

Speak Kindly to Yourself:

When that inner critic starts to shout, remind yourself: "If I wouldn't say it to a friend, I don't need to say it to myself." Remember that kindness is a form of strength, not a weakness.

Connect When You Want to Withdraw:

Reach out to someone you trust. Sending even a single message can help shatter the isolation that so often accompanies difficult times. You don't have to carry it alone.

Choose One Thing:

When everything feels overwhelming, focus on just one small action. Whether it's washing your face, stepping outside, or writing a single sentence, remember that every little step counts. It doesn't have to be monumental; it just needs to be yours.

Reflection Prompt: Embrace Your Inner Strength

Think about a challenging experience you've survived that you once thought would defeat you. What insights did that experience reveal about your strength and resilience?

Think back to a significant moment in your life that felt like it might break you. Yet here you are, still standing. What did that experience teach you about your ability to adapt, endure, and grow?

Use the space on this page to explore:
- What strengths did you discover in that moment?
- What would you say to the version of yourself who made it through?

This is how resilience flourishes, not through striving for perfection, but through embracing the present. You don't have to have all the answers. Just keep showing up for yourself, one breath, one truth, one healing moment at a time. Each step is a testament to your strength.

My Mind Doesn't Sit Still – Living with ADHD

People often misunderstand ADHD, viewing it as merely being fidgety or forgetful. They picture a person who is loud, constantly bouncing off the walls, or perpetually losing their keys. But for me, ADHD is so much more complex. It's like having a thousand tabs open in my brain, each one struggling to load fully, each urging for my attention, but none completely resolving.

It's the relentless desire to focus, yet feeling tethered by an invisible weight that pulls my mind in every direction. It's being deeply invested in my responsibilities, yet consistently missing deadlines due to the chaotic whirlpool of thoughts. When I hear people say "just try harder," I feel a wave of frustration wash over me. If raw effort were the solution, I'd have found my cure long ago.

Living with the Chaos

ADHD is far from a mere quirk; it often feels like an intense, daily workout for the mind. For me, living with ADHD manifests in various, overwhelming ways:

- I can be daunted by simple tasks, yet find myself fiercely hyper focused on something seemingly trivial at 2 AM, my mind racing with thoughts.
- I frequently forget appointments and obligations, only to be consumed by guilt and anxiety afterward, wondering if I've let others down.
- Despite my deep desire for routine and structure, I regularly struggle to implement it, feeling as though I'm swimming against the current.
- I engage in constant self-correction, battling the internal voices that remind me: "Stop talking so much," "Stay on track," "Don't interrupt," creating a mental tug-of-war that is exhausting.
- It often leaves me feeling paradoxical: both too much and not enough, leading to a cycle of exhaustion not only for me but for the version of myself desperately trying to mask these struggles.

86

The Frustration No One Sees

ADHD can feel like an internal conflict of motivation without clear direction, bubbling ideas that fail to materialize into action, and battling against the relentless tide of self-doubt, despite my best efforts.

- I struggle with starting tasks but find it difficult to finish them, not due to laziness, but rather because my attention can switch unexpectedly mid-task, leaving me disoriented.
- I often find myself speaking too quickly, moving restlessly, or caught in a loop of repetitive thoughts, which can be disheartening.
- Then comes the inevitable crash, sometimes I accomplish everything in one burst of energy, only to feel completely drained afterward, or end up doing nothing at all, lost in indecision.

The Guilt That Lingers

- I frequently wrestle with guilt over my perceived failures.
- I berate myself when I forget important things or when I impulsively speak before considering my words.
- There's a familiar shame that washes over me when I leave messages unread, not because I didn't care to respond, but simply because my mind skipped over it entirely.
- The most painful part is the lingering feeling of disappointment, constantly worrying that I'm letting down those around me, or worse, letting myself down.

How I Started Understanding It

Receiving a diagnosis was not just a label; it was an awakening. It provided me with a lens through which I could finally understand my unique brain wiring.

- It illuminated the fact that I wasn't broken; I was simply different, which helped diminish the self-judgment I'd been harbouring for so long.
- I began to explore concepts like executive dysfunction, dopamine regulation, and emotional dysregulation, realizing that these weren't just quirks, they were integral parts of my experience with ADHD, reshaping how I viewed myself.

What's Helped Me (So Far)

- I'm still on this journey, but several strategies have proven helpful:

- Utilizing timers and visual cues has been invaluable, as my "I'll do it later" often translates to "I'll forget it exists."
- Engaging in body doubling, having someone present while I work provides grounding and helps me stay focused and accountable.
- I've learned to break tasks down into manageable micro-steps; instead of thinking I need to "clean the entire house," I remind myself that I can "clear the coffee table" first, making the task feel less daunting.
- I practice compassionate self-talk: I replace harsh criticism like "you're useless" with kinder reminders: "You're learning to navigate your brain's unique path, not fighting against it."
- Medication has been a significant consideration, while it's a transformative option for some, it may not work for everyone, but it's definitely worth exploring.

If You're Reading This...

I want you to know: you're not lazy. You're not careless. You're not a mess. You're a human being navigating a world that often overlooks the intricacies of neurodivergent minds. ADHD isn't about lack of effort, it's about working ten times harder than most realize, yet still feeling misunderstood.

Within your mind lies immense strength, creativity, and a vibrant energy that can propel you forward. With the right tools, compassionate support, and kindness to yourself, you have the potential not just to survive but to truly thrive.

Personal Reflection: Practical Tools for Gentle Self-Compassion

Living with ADHD can often feel like trying to navigate a world that feels misaligned with your unique brain. It's important to remember that this journey isn't about simply trying harder; it's about figuring out how to support yourself in different ways. Self-compassion isn't just a nice-to-have, it's essential for your well-being.

Here are a few gentle tools that I've found helpful; think of them as possibilities rather than prescriptions:

Micro-Steps Over Master Plans

Large tasks can often seem overwhelming. Take a breath and try to break things down into the tiniest of steps. Instead of thinking "clean the house," focus on just "put one mug in the sink." Start small, and allow that momentum to grow at your own pace.

Timers & External Cues

It's easy to lose track of time and tasks when they're out of sight. Consider using phone reminders, sticky notes, or visual timers. This isn't a sign of weakness; it's a clever strategy to help you stay on track.

Body Doubling

If you can, invite someone to be near you while you work, even if it's just virtually. There's no need for conversation, their presence can provide a comforting sense of shared focus.

Name the ADHD Narrative

When your inner critic pipes up with thoughts like "you're lazy" or "you can't stay on track," take a moment to pause and gently reframe those thoughts. Instead, try saying to yourself: "I'm not lazy; my brain just needs a different kind of pacing." Or, "I'm not broken; I'm uniquely wired."

Explore Medication Without Shame

If medication is part of your journey, know that it's not a shortcut, it's a valuable support system. Honouring this choice doesn't take away from your efforts; it complements them.

Reflection Prompt: Living with (and Not Against) ADHD

Consider this: What aspects of your ADHD do you struggle with the most? And, if you dig deep, what parts of it do you secretly cherish?

ADHD isn't solely a challenge; it's a relationship. With yourself, your time, your attention, and your emotions. Take a moment for some quiet reflection:

What aspects of ADHD do you find most challenging, focus, follow-through, emotional regulation, routine?
Now, take a closer look: What parts of your ADHD truly make you who you are? Is it your creativity? Your curiosity? Your intense passion when something captivates your interest?

Write down your thoughts freely, with honesty and compassion toward yourself. Remember, you are not a problem to fix, you're a complex person seeking understanding, and this journey begins with you.

The Fire That Fades – Living with Burnout

Burnout is often misunderstood. It doesn't always manifest as a dramatic collapse where one falls to the floor in utter exhaustion. Instead, it can resemble a quiet façade of functionality, answering emails, smiling through meetings, preparing dinner for loved ones, while internally, you feel like a flickering lightbulb on the brink of extinguishing. For a long time, I mistook my symptoms as mere tiredness or a lack of motivation, thinking I was simply failing to meet the expectations of life. What I was truly enduring, however, was profound emotional, physical, and mental depletion years spent operating on autopilot in a constant state of survival.

What Burnout Really Feels Like

Burnout is distinctly different from regular stress; whereas stress often feels like being overwhelmed by an excessive load, burnout translates to an utter depletion of resources. It's waking up and feeling a persistent, hollow echo of exhaustion that a good night's sleep cannot remedy. In my experience, burnout manifested in several troubling ways:

- Loss of Passion: I found myself detached from activities and hobbies I once cherished, leaving me feeling listless and uninspired.
- Cognitive Fog: Concentration became a struggle; after only a few minutes of focus, my mind would spiral into a thick haze, making even basic tasks seem insurmountable.
- Disconnection: Despite being surrounded by loved ones, I often felt a profound sense of disconnect. Conversations felt shallow, and I struggled to engage emotionally.
- Mountains of Simple Tasks: Even the smallest responsibilities, such as replying to a text or folding laundry, felt like Herculean tasks that drained every ounce of my energy.
- Unexplained Emotions: I experienced tears without understanding the cause, and at other times, I felt completely numb, unable to cry at all, heightening my sense of isolation.

Doubts plagued my mind: "Maybe I'm just not cut out for this," or "Perhaps I'm the problem." However, the truth was I was simply exhausted, pushed beyond my limits without the recognition of how deeply this exhaustion ran.

The Hidden Toll

Burnout often sneaks in gradually, camouflaging itself as a necessary endurance. We push ourselves because we feel an obligation, to our jobs, families, and households. We tell ourselves, "Just get through today," but over time, this relentless pursuit chips away at our emotional reserves. The consequences are profound: emotional numbness, detachment, and a disconnection from one's self and one's feelings.

The effects of burnout extended to my relationships and self-perception. I became irritable and short-tempered, snapping at family and friends who hadn't changed but whose patience wore thin under my strain. My sleep patterns became erratic, sometimes filled with restless nights and other times, I would sleep too much, desperately seeking escape in dreams. I began to dread things that once brought me joy, feeling constantly overstimulated yet emotionally flat, a paradox that intensified my feelings of inadequacy.

Burnout is not a sign of laziness; it's a clarion call from your body and mind, a way of saying, "Enough is enough."

How I Realised I Was Burnt Out

Initially, I directed my frustrations inward, convinced that the answer lay in working harder, improving my organization, or squeezing more from my daily schedule. But no productivity hacks, time management strategies, or meticulously crafted to-do lists could rescue me from the emotional spiral. The real turning point came when I shifted my approach from forced resilience to active listening to myself.

I made the crucial admission that I simply wasn't okay. I began to take decisive steps to care for my well-being:

- I started cancelling social engagements, allowing myself to do so without guilt, recognizing that prioritizing rest was essential for my healing.
- I stepped back from commitments that felt overwhelmingly draining, understanding that it was okay to carve out time for self-care.

- I began to ask myself, "What do I genuinely need in this moment?" This introspection became a lifeline, guiding me toward small steps of recovery.

What Helped Me (So Far)

1. Daily Check-Ins: Each day, I made it a point to check in with myself by asking, "How is my energy today?" This simple question helped me acknowledge my exhaustion instead of ignoring it.

2. Setting Boundaries: I learned to say no, not only to others but also to the inner voice that insisted on constant busyness and productivity.

3. Permission to Rest: I embraced rest without guilt, allowing myself to nap when necessary and understanding that rest is a fundamental human need, not something to be earned.

4. Joy Breaks: I reintroduced small, meaningful moments of joy into my life, whether it was watching the sunset, savouring a warm cup of tea, or cuddling with my pets. These were moments that grounded me and reminded me of the beauty in everyday life.

5. Reconnection: I reached out to friends and family, not with a polished update but with raw honesty: "I'm struggling. Can we talk?" This vulnerability helped me rebuild connections that felt frayed.

If You're Reading This...

If you find yourself resonating with these words, know this: you are not lazy, unmotivated, or a failure. You are tired, and your fatigue is entirely valid. Your self-worth is not defined by your productivity or the balance you maintain among life's demands. It is perfectly acceptable to fall apart, to pause, and to embark on the journey of starting over slowly, at your own pace.

Personal Reflection: Embracing Gentle Self-Compassion

The "Bare Minimum" List: Take a moment to identify three non-negotiable things that nurture your wellbeing. For me, it's staying hydrated, taking my medication, and stepping outside for just five minutes. On particularly tough days, accomplishing these three small acts can be more than enough.

Energy Mapping: Consider keeping a simple log to observe when your energy tends to rise or fall throughout the day. This can provide valuable insights and help you plan your tasks with greater compassion for yourself.

The Stoplight System: Try using a color-coded approach to assess your capacity for the day:
- Red: I need to fully rest.
- Yellow: I can manage light tasks, but I'll need breaks.
- Green: I'm ready to tackle my regular commitments. Allow this system to guide your day, freeing you from guilt.

Create a "No" Script: It can be helpful to prepare a few gentle phrases to say no without feeling the need to explain yourself. Here are some examples:
- "I appreciate you thinking of me, but I need to decline."
- "I'm at my limit right now."

Reflection Prompt: Reclaiming Your Spark

Think about three small things that bring you comfort or peace, even if it's just for a moment. Write them down, and then reflect on when you last allowed yourself to enjoy these without feeling guilty.

Now, let's craft a sentence of permission for yourself. Start with: "It is okay for me to rest because..." Keep this phrase visible as a gentle reminder that experiencing burnout is not a personal failure. It signifies that you have been incredibly strong for too long, often without support. Remember, you truly deserve your own loving care, too.

When the Past Won't Stay in the Past – Living with Complex Post Traumatic Stress Disorder (CPTSD)

There are two distinct types of trauma: one that knocks you down with a single blow, and another that steadily erodes your sense of self over time. This slow chipping away is what defines Complex Post-Traumatic Stress Disorder (CPTSD). Unlike a sudden event that leaves you reeling, CPTSD is experienced as a thousand cumulative moments, each one contributing to a profound sense of disconnection from your own identity.

Imagine emotional neglect that lingers like a shadow, the feeling of repeated abandonment that festers, chronic fear that infiltrates your thoughts, and a love so unstable that you never know which version of "safe" will greet you each day. For a long time, I didn't even recognize that I was dealing with trauma; I simply believed I was too sensitive, too reactive, and irrevocably broken.

What CPTSD Feels Like (From the Inside)

CPTSD is more than just flashbacks, it's a web of patterns that intertwine with my daily life. My nervous system has become hyper-aware; I flinch at gestures of affection or warmth, sabotaging closeness with the expectation that those I care about will eventually leave. Conversations from the past loop in my mind, morphing into feelings of shame that linger. Each day can feel like a minefield of emotions, where I'm perpetually on guard and over-analysing every interaction, shutting down emotionally when things get overwhelming. I oscillate between feeling "too much" and "not enough," struggling to trust even in safe environments.

This is not melodrama; this is my daily existence.

Why It's "Complex"

Unlike PTSD, which often stems from a single traumatic event, CPTSD emerges from a lifetime of instability, characterized by unsafe attachments and conditional love. I learned to read moods before mastering the vocabulary of words. I became adept at suppressing my own needs just to maintain peace, avoiding conflict at all costs while silently blaming myself for the pain inflicted by others. This became my survival mechanism, a way to navigate a world that felt chaotic. Now, I'm engaged in the challenging work of unlearning those behaviours.

The Reactions That Don't Make Sense (Until They Do)

People often inquire, "Why do you overreact?" Yet, they remain unaware of the vast iceberg hidden beneath the surface of my reactions. My silence serves as a shield, protecting me from further harm. My anger often disguises deep-seated fear, and when I choose to push people away, it's because my caring for them is intertwined with an intense fear of being hurt again. The manifestations of CPTSD are felt within my body, manifesting as a racing heart, a tightening in my chest, and a sense of fatigue after even the simplest interactions. Out in public, I am on high alert, yet when I'm alone, I may completely shut down, only to be burdened by the guilt of feeling so much.

The Loops I Get Stuck In

I often find myself caught in cycles of people-pleasing, where the desire to be liked outweighs the need for honesty. I shut down emotionally because vulnerability has historically equated to punishment. I over-apologize, conditioned to believe that I am at fault for others' emotions or behaviours. Even resting becomes a struggle, as survival has ingrained in me the belief that stillness is a threat. These behaviours are not inherent flaws; they are coping mechanisms I developed during times of helplessness. However, I recognize now that these strategies have begun to harm me, and I am committed to healing them.

What's Helping Me Reclaim My Life

Healing from CPTSD is anything but linear. It's a journey that is often slow, messy, and painful, yet it is also entirely possible. Some of the strategies that help me include:
- Naming my trauma instead of keeping it hidden away
- Establishing safe routines that soothe my nervous system
- Representing myself in moments when my inner child feels overwhelmed
- Engaging in therapy, particularly trauma-informed approaches like EMDR or somatic therapy

- Learning to experience emotions in a safe, non-judgmental manner

There are still times when I shut down, but I'm becoming more adept at recognizing those moments. I take a breath, centre myself, and allow my awareness to return a little quicker each time.

If You've Ever Thought "I'm Just Damaged" ...

You're not damaged. You adapted to pain in ways that were inherently brave. Now, as you strive to adapt to peace, understand that this requires an even greater courage. CPTSD didn't make you weak; instead, it has cultivated sensitivity, heightened awareness, and a fierce protectiveness within you. The goal now is to transform those traits into powerful tools for healing rather than mere survival responses.

Personal Reflection: Practical Tools for Gentle Self-Compassion

Living with Complex PTSD is not a personal weakness. It is the nervous system's answer to prolonged stress, threat, or neglect. Healing does not happen overnight. It requires patience, grounding, and compassion. The tools below are rooted in trauma-informed and evidence-based methods used by psychologists and counsellors. They are not meant to fix you. They are meant to help you live gently with the parts of you that never felt safe enough to rest.

1. Use Psychoeducation to Understand Yourself

In trauma-informed therapy, the very first step is to understand what trauma does to the mind and body .
Try this:
Learn one thing each week about how CPTSD shows up, for example, nervous system dysregulation, emotional flashbacks, or dissociation.
Write that discovery down with a note: "This is what's happening. This is not broken. It is survival."

2. Build Bottom-Up Grounding Practices

Therapies for complex trauma encourage body-based tools to reconnect nervous systems
Try this:

- **Body scan**: Place your attention on your feet, then legs, moving upward. Notice tension or warmth without changing it.
- **Somatic pause**: Place a hand on your heart, feel your breath, and pause for ten seconds. Allow your system to notice you are safe now.

3. Practice Narrative Exposure with Compassion

Narrative Exposure Therapy helps to organize traumatic memories within a broader life story
Try this:
Use a journal to map your lifeline: mark positive events as leaves or flowers, more difficult events as stones. You don't need to dive into the hardest memories now. Just frame them as part of your journey.

4. Reframe Through Cognitive Processing Therapy (CPT)

CPT is a structured method to challenge trauma-shaped beliefs.
Try this:
Pick one belief that arose from trauma, such as "I am powerless."
Ask:

- What evidence supports this?
- What evidence opposes it?
- Is there a middle way?
  Rewrite it into something more balanced, like "I faced danger before. Now I can choose what to face."

5. Integrate Trauma-Focused CBT Tools

Trauma-focused CBT uses exposure and coping skills to rebuild emotional tolerance.
Try this:
List small things you've been avoiding, for example, driving through busy streets, or talking about a past hurt. Pick the easiest one. Imagine doing it calmly. Then when ready try it slowly, one step at a time, with self-kindness.

6. Try Somatic Experiencing for Sensory Reconnection

Somatic Experiencing helps release stored stress through awareness of physical sensations .

Try this:
After a moment that felt intense, tension, racing thoughts, freeze response, pause.
Ask your body: where did that emotion land?
Observe the sensation quietly without rushing. Let your body find its own resolution.

7. Use Mindfulness to Build Emotional Regulation

Mindfulness techniques have been shown to reduce trauma symptoms by fostering interoception
Try this:
Use a mindfulness anchor, breath, sound, touch. When distress arises, pause and gently bring your attention back to the anchor. Aim for 1–2 minutes per day and build from there.

8. Explore EMDR-Inspired Bilateral Attention

EMDR uses bilateral stimulation to help reprocess trauma memories.
Try this (self-guided):
Recall a neutral, comforting memory.
Gently move your eyes side to side, or tap your legs alternately.
Notice what shifts in your body or mind. This is not full EMDR but can gently soothe.

9. Ground Yourself with Ritual and Routine

Trauma-informed care emphasizes safety, trust, and empowerment as core principles
Try this:
Before any challenging task, honour your system with a ritual: a grounding breath, lighting a candle, adjusting lighting. Signals to your nervous system that it is safe to engage.

10. Cultivate a Safe Relationship with Yourself

Strong therapeutic relationships support healing
Try this:
Each day, reassure yourself as a compassionate friend would, especially

when you feel triggered or lost. Let self-talk be the anchor of empathy and trust in yourself.

Reflection Prompt

List one pattern you use to survive, avoidance, perfectionism, people-pleasing. How did it help you at first? What does it cost you now?

Choose one new tool above. Try it this week. Afterward, note what you felt, not what you fixed. Just felt.

End with gratitude for your survival and curiosity for your healing. You are not broken. You are here. You are brave at every breath.

The Storm and the Silence: Living with Bipolar Disorder

For years, I navigated the tumultuous waters of my emotions without a compass. I struggled to articulate what I felt, lumping my experiences into vague descriptors like "erratic," "unpredictable," or simply "too intense." Some days, I soared with an electrifying energy, flooded with ideas, and brimming with confidence, feeling as if I could conquer the world. Other days, I sank into a deep abyss, finding the smallest tasks, like brushing my teeth, overwhelmingly daunting. During those moments, I questioned my worth and competence, believing I was somehow failing at life. It wasn't until I began to educate myself about bipolar disorder that I discovered I wasn't broken. I was merely misunderstood, even by myself.

Understanding Bipolar Disorder

Bipolar disorder is often misunderstood and misrepresented in popular culture as merely a series of mood swings. In reality, it is a multifaceted mental health condition characterized by significant and often unpredictable shifts in emotional states. Such swings typically fall between two poles: mania (or hypomania) and depression and each phase embodies its own distinct challenges and experiences.

Mania and Hypomania: The Highs

During a manic or hypomanic episode, life feels electric. It manifests as an internal fire, igniting racing thoughts and leading to sleepless nights filled with projects and ideas that seem brilliant. There's an exhilarating sense of limitless ambition and confidence, making grand plans feel achievable, and a euphoric belief in one's own invincibility. However, this state often carries an underlying irritability, where one might react strongly to perceived slights, feeling as though the world isn't moving fast enough to match their heightened energy.

Depression: The Lows

Conversely, depression during the low phases feels like a heavy shroud has descended, everything slows down to a halt, and hopelessness becomes a constant companion. Activities that once brought joy now seem colourless and dull, leading to a disinterest that drains the spirit. Feelings of guilt and shame permeate this state too, as one reflects on actions taken or not taken during the energetic times, creating a painful juxtaposition between moments of brilliance and despair.

These experiences are not mere mood shifts; they are profound states that can disrupt daily life, affecting work, relationships, sleep patterns, self-trust, and personal identity. The confusing nature of these shifts can leave one in a state of constant anticipation, braced for the next wave of emotional turmoil.

Navigating Everyday Life with Bipolar Disorder

Living with bipolar disorder often requires finding the words to describe the indescribable. I became aware of this disorder's patterns in my life, noticing how it manifested in various ways:

- I would dive into multiple creative projects, bursting with enthusiasm, only to abandon them shortly after, overwhelmed by the chaos and feeling deep shame for my inability to follow through.
- I'd indulge in impulsive spending or make grandiose plans, full of conviction that they were brilliant, only to be left reeling in regret when the manic energy waned.
- Periods of sleeplessness fuelled by excitement would often lead to crushing fatigue, leaving me unable to engage in social situations or articulate thoughts clearly.
- Friends and family would celebrate the energy and creativity I exhibited during my hypomanic phases, yet they remained oblivious to the inevitable crash that followed, as well as the harsh self-criticism I faced in the aftermath.

It would often feel as if I were two distinct individuals inhabiting the same body, one filled with dreams and aspirations, the other weighed down in silence and stillness, each vying for acknowledgment and space.

Understanding the Bipolar Spectrum

Bipolar disorder encompasses different types, each with unique characteristics:

- Bipolar I Disorder features full manic episodes, which may be severe enough to require hospitalization and are usually accompanied by depressive episodes.

- Bipolar II Disorder includes hypomanic episodes, milder than full mania—alongside longer, more persistent depressive states.
- Cyclothymiacs involves alternating periods of hypomanic and depressive symptoms that don't meet full diagnostic criteria but still significantly disrupt daily life.

The causes are not simply rooted in a "chemical imbalance." Instead, they arise from a complex interplay of genetic predisposition, neurobiological factors, emotional sensitivity, past traumas, and environmental stressors. For many individuals, receiving a diagnosis brings a sense of relief, a framework that helps clarify years of confusion and struggle.

Learning to Coexist with Bipolar Disorder

Recognizing and accepting my diagnosis didn't provide an instant solution; however, it equipped me with a vocabulary, a toolkit for navigating my internal landscape. By acknowledging the patterns instead of assigning blame to myself, I started cultivating awareness rather than pursuing an unattainable ideal of consistency. Managing bipolar disorder became less about resisting its duality and more about creating a life that accommodates both the energy of mania and the quietude of depression.

Personal Reflection: Embracing All Versions of Myself

There was a point in my journey where I dreaded the extremes of my personality, the soaring highs and crushing lows. Looking back at photos from those elevated phases, I often felt disconnected, as if I was observing an actor playing a role rather than looking at my authentic self. However, through reflection and acceptance, I've started recognizing both ends of my emotional spectrum not as adversaries, but as integral parts of my identity. Each embodies a facet of me, each trying to protect, express, or escape something deep within.

I am learning to nurture both the high-flying version of myself, gently reminding her that "It's okay to take things down a notch," and to embrace the quieter, more reflective version with the reassurance, "You are still worthy, even in your stillness."

Practical Tools for Bipolar Regulation

While these tools don't serve as cures, they act as anchors to help ground, regulate, and support my journey through this complex landscape:

1. Mood Tracking: I maintain a simple daily mood tracker, often using colours or emoji to chart my sleep, energy, thoughts, and behaviours. This allows me to identify emerging patterns before they escalate into crises.

2. Anchor Routines: Establishing consistent sleep/wake times, meal schedules, and screen time boundaries helps stabilize my nervous system, particularly during vulnerable transitions.

3. Creative Outlets: In periods of heightened energy, I channel my creativity through writing, sketching, or recording voice notes to capture the influx of inspiration without impulsively acting on every whim.

4. Crisis Plans: I have developed a comprehensive safety plan for times when I feel myself tipping into an emotional downturn. This plan includes a trusted contact I can reach out to, a detailed medication protocol, and a calming note I crafted during a peaceful moment.

5. Permission to Rest: I remind myself that rest is not a sign of laziness; rather, it serves as a necessary preventative measure, allowing me to maintain balance and avoid burnout.

By incorporating these practices into my life, I continue to learn the importance of embracing the full spectrum of my experience, both the storms and the periods of silence, shaping my journey into one of acceptance, resilience, and self-discovery.

Personal Reflection: Practical Tools for Gentle Self-Compassion

Living with bipolar disorder isn't about trying to "fix" yourself; it's about the journey of learning to meet yourself right where you are, time and again, without placing any weight of shame on your shoulders.

It's essential to recognize that we can't control the currents of our emotions and experiences. However, we can discover ways to navigate those waves with more grace, preparation, and kindness towards ourselves. Here are some nurturing tools I lean on, gentle anchors that help me stay connected to myself, especially during overwhelming or unpredictable times:

Mood Mapping as Self-Awareness, Not Self-Judgment

Consider a daily check-in using colour codes, emoji's, numbers, or brief notes. This practice isn't about labelling days as "good" or "bad." Instead, it's an opportunity to notice your feelings and experiences with a compassionate lens. Think of it as a way to observe, not as a scorecard that you have to compete against.

Grounding Routines Over Rigid Schedules

Rather than imposing strict schedules on yourself, strive for predictable moments in your day. Establish gentle rituals, such as your wake-up routine, wind-down cues, or nourishing meals. These can serve as safe touchpoints, especially when internal chaos makes the external world feel uncertain.

Creative Containers

When you're experiencing bursts of energy, find safe spaces for your ideas to rest. This could be through voice notes, a "Big Ideas" notebook, or a sketchpad. Allow your creativity to flow without the pressure to act on every thought. Remember, not every spark needs to ignite into a blaze.

Create a 'Low Day' Toolkit

When depression sets in, it's easy to forget what helps you. Consider putting together a small list of gentle reminders, like:
- "Drink water."
- "Open a window."
- "Message this person."
- "Listen to that calming playlist."

This isn't about fixing the mood; it's about nurturing yourself while you navigate it.

Talk to Yourself Like You're Worth Saving

Both the manic and depressive sides of yourself deserve compassion. Try reaching out to your inner self with affirming words like:
- "You're safe."
- "You've felt this way before—and you made it through."
- "You don't need to earn your rest."

- "You're still you, even on hard days."

These affirmations may not resolve the storm, but they can help keep your inner world afloat.

Reflection Prompt: Holding Both Versions of You

Reflect on a time you were caught in a manic or depressive state, and do so without judgment. Consider these questions:
- What was that part of you trying to communicate or protect?
- What needs lay beneath that behaviour, were they for connection, control, expression, or rest?
- How can you approach yourself differently next time, not to correct, but to comfort?

Write a message to both versions of yourself. Perhaps start with:
- "To the part of me that rises like lightning…"
- "To the part of me that sinks like stone…"

Remind them that both versions are valid and allowed to coexist. They both deserve grace, and you are worthy of peace, not just during moments of balance, but always.

The Ghosts from Before – Understanding Childhood Trauma

I didn't always recognize what I was dealing with, thinking it was merely a matter of being sensitive, difficult, or somehow inadequate. For years, I believed that my emotional responses were just quirks of my personality. It took time to understand that the memories I had buried the experiences I was told to overlook, were still very much alive within me, orchestrating my thoughts and actions from the shadows.

These past experiences moulded my reactions, instilled fears, coloured my relationships, and influenced my sense of self-worth. They played like an incessant loop of background music that I couldn't switch off, subtly leading me to question my reality, my feelings, and my place in the world.

What Childhood Trauma Really Is

Childhood trauma often deviates from the typical narratives of violence or overt dysfunction. It can manifest in more insidious ways, including:

- The deafening silence that follows your tears, where comfort was absent.
- Moments of neglect when you reached for support that never came.
- A pervasive sense that love and affection had to be earned rather than freely given.
- Growing up prematurely because no one safeguarded your innocence from harsh realities.
- Carrying emotional burdens that were never yours to bear, transforming your childhood into a cycle of adult responsibilities far too early.

Trauma is not defined solely by external events; it revolves around your internal experience. It's not about how "bad" things appeared on the surface but rather, how profoundly unsafe you felt within. If it continues to hurt, it undoubtedly mattered.

How It Shows Up Now

You would think that trauma remains confined to the past. However, it seeps into the present day, embedding itself in your nervous system, influencing relationships, and dictating choices.

- I began to notice its presence when:
- I would flinch at raised voices, even when they weren't directed at me, a remnant of fear echoing from the past.
- I found myself apologizing for actions that had nothing to do with me, as if I was responsible for the emotions of others.
- I struggled to trust acts of kindness, always questioning the motives behind them.
- I oscillated between feeling utterly numb and overwhelmed, as though my emotions were on a pendulum of extremes.
- Small, everyday occurrences felt like major threats, leading to self-loathing for what I perceived as overreactions.

Looking back, I learned that I was never truly overreacting; I was merely re-living a past experience that had shaped my current reactions.

Introducing the ABC Model

(The ABC (adversity, behavior, consequences) model is one of the main parts of rational emotive behavior therapy (REBT), a form of cognitive behavioral therapy (CBT). 1 The ABC model is based on the idea that emotions and behaviors are not determined by external events but by our beliefs about them.)

One tool that significantly clarified my experience was the ABC Model. It presents a straightforward yet effective framework that was transformative for my mental health.

A = Adversity: This is what happens, whether it's from the past or present—a trigger such as a certain tone of voice or being left without a response.

B = Behaviour: After the activating event, your mind assigns meaning to it, often shaped by childhood experiences. I would find myself thinking, "I'm not good enough," or "People always leave," or "I need to fix this."

C = Consequence: The beliefs lead to emotional and behavioural consequences, such as feelings of panic, withdrawal, an urge to please others, or shutting down completely.

As I began using this model, it became a map for navigating my emotional reactions. Instead of harshly judging myself, I learned to cultivate curiosity:

- What was the activating event? (A)
- What story did I tell myself in response? (B)
- How did I act or feel because of that story? (C)

Often, I discovered that my beliefs were outdated—remnants of a childhood fear that still haunted me.

Rewriting the Script

Through consistent practice, I started to transform my inner narrative. Instead of spiralling into thoughts like, "They're angry; I must've done something wrong," I moved toward a more balanced perspective: "Their emotions are valid; it doesn't mean I am at fault."

Similarly, instead of thinking, "They haven't replied to my message; they must hate me," I learned to counter with, "My anxiety is creating a story based on incomplete information. I don't know the full picture."

This transformative process wasn't instantaneous. It required patience and intentional effort over time. Slowly but surely, I began to feel more secure within myself, fundamentally altering how I interacted with the world.

A Word on Safety

If your upbringing steered you into survival mode, you may find yourself perpetually trapped in that mind-set. Constantly scanning for potential threats, struggling to relax, and feeling a need to control every detail just to experience a moment of peace is exhausting.

But true safety does not arise from control; it emerges from deep-seated compassion. It involves acknowledging your experiences and saying to yourself, "I see you. I hear you. You didn't deserve what happened to you. Together, we will heal."

That "we"? It's the connection between your adult self and your inner child, embarking on a journey of understanding and healing together.

Personal Reflection: The Child I Left Behind

There was a time when I believed my childhood experiences were just "fine." I had food on the table, a roof over my head, and I wasn't physically harmed or confined. So, how could I ever claim to be traumatized? That word felt too heavy, too significant for someone like me, someone who seemed to have the basic necessities.

However, I've come to understand that trauma isn't solely about the overt actions or events in our lives. It can also stem from what was absent, what we never received.

I didn't fully grasp how deeply silence had shaped my experience. There was the silence that followed when I was labelled as "too sensitive," a phrase that silenced my emotions. The silence that enveloped me when I cried, and no one noticed or responded. The silence during moments when I desperately needed comfort but was met with demands to "toughen up." In those moments, I learned to swallow my feelings, stifling them before they could be dismissed or belittled. I learned to shrink myself down to fit the comfort of others around me.

That child, moulded by those experiences, quiet, anxious, and frequently apologizing continued to shadow me into adulthood.

Even now, I occasionally catch myself flinching at acts of kindness or preparing for inevitable disappointment. It's almost as though that inner child still believes that love must be meticulously earned through a facade of perfection, that expressing vulnerability is inherently risky, and that asking for help equates to being a burden.

Yet, the profound truth I'm gradually embracing is this: that child didn't need to toughen up. What they truly needed was to feel a sense of safety. They needed someone anyone to assure them, "You're allowed to feel what you feel." Now, as an adult, I realize that I possess the power to be that nurturing figure for myself.

Healing doesn't erase the past; rather, it rewrites the narratives that have been imposed on us. It teaches me that I wasn't "too much." I was simply "too alone," grappling with feelings that no one equipped me to handle.

Practical Tools for Inner Child Healing

Inner Child Letter

Take the time to write a heartfelt letter to your younger self, focusing on the age when you first felt unsafe or invisible. Use simple, kind language that resonates with that child's understanding. Express the words and sentiments they never received. After you've penned it, read the letter aloud to yourself. Allow yourself to feel the catharsis and the weight lift as you convey those long-overdue sentiments.

Safe Space Visualization

Find a quiet space and close your eyes. Picture a place where your inner child feels utterly safe and secure, this might be a cosy room, a lush garden, or an enchanting realm of your imagination. Envision yourself sitting beside them, holding their tiny hand, assuring them with your presence that you are here now and that you will not abandon them.

Gentle Re-Parenting Mantra

Create a personal mantra, a comforting phrase to repeat when your inner critic surfaces. It could be something empowering like:
- "I'm allowed to take up space."
- "I don't need to earn love."
- "My feelings are valid and safe with me."

Utilize this mantra in moments of shame, fear, or when those old wounds resurface.

Practical Tools for Nurturing Self-Compassion

Healing from childhood trauma can feel overwhelming, and it often begins not with grand epiphanies, but with gentle, intentional moments of remembrance. It's about recognizing not only the memories themselves but also the deep impacts they've had on you. Acknowledge those parts of yourself that had to grow up too quickly, the parts that still shrink away from kindness, and those that never truly understood what safety felt like.

These tools won't magically resolve everything, but they can be the first steps toward starting anew. Together with your inner child, you can begin to heal and nurture that relationship.

1. Write to Your Inner Child

Take a moment of quiet for yourself. Write a heartfelt letter to the child you once were, speaking with kindness and love. Share the words and affirmations that may have been absent in their life. Allow your adult self to become the source of comfort and reassurance they've always needed.

2. Safe Space Visualization

Close your eyes and envision your inner child in a safe and serene place, perhaps a peaceful beach, a cosy bed, or a luminous forest. See yourself there beside them, holding their hand tightly. Remind them softly, "You are safe now. I'm here for you."

3. Gentle Re-Parenting Mantra

Create a comforting phrase to repeat when feelings of shame or self-doubt arise. Phrases like:
- "I am allowed to feel."
- "I don't have to be perfect to be loved."
- "I will continue to care for myself."

Say these often, allowing them to wrap around you like a warm blanket, nurturing your spirit.

Prompt:

Reflect on a recent moment that triggered you. Consider the following:

- What was the Activating Event?
- What Belief surfaced in response?
- What was the Consequence? how did you feel, or how did you act?

Then ask yourself: Is there a different, kinder belief I could choose instead? This process of reflection can foster growth and pave the way for healthier emotional responses.

Reflect on a moment from your childhood when you felt fear, neglect, or misunderstanding. If you could travel back in time and sit beside your younger self, what would you say? What words would provide them the comfort they desperately needed? Write it out and let them hear your voice now.

Reflection Prompt: Rewriting the Past with Compassion

Think back to a specific moment in your childhood when you felt unseen, scared, or misunderstood. Now picture your adult self-sitting beside you in that moment. What would you say to that younger version of yourself? How would you comfort them? What do they need to hear from you right now?

Use the space provided to write them a letter. Speak to them with gentleness and honesty. This is your opportunity to begin offering them the love and care they always deserved.

Remember to check in with yourself and your emotions at this moment in time.

Healing the Inner Child – A Workbook for CPTSD Recovery

I didn't realize I was still carrying them, the younger versions of me. The little one who felt invisible, who blended into the background, striving to be unnoticed to avoid conflict. The one who flinched at the slightest hint of anger, conditioned to fear outbursts that felt like thunderclaps in a quiet room. The one who desperately tried to earn love and acceptance by being perfect, believing that if I just achieved enough or behaved well enough, I would finally be worthy of affection.

But they were still there, living within me, rooted in my anxiety, manifesting in my sudden emotional shutdowns, lurking in my irrational fear of being "too much" for others to handle. As I embarked on my journey of healing from Complex PTSD, I learned that healing meant more than just time passing; it meant actively recognizing these inner children, truly hearing their needs, and finally protecting them in ways that no one else had. It was a journey of deep compassion, one that required courage and patience.

This chapter isn't just for reading. It's a call to action, a personal invitation for you to engage deeply with your own healing process. There's no need to rush. Take your time and embrace the messiness of your emotions. Let it be a journey that belongs entirely to you.

Section 1: Meet Your Inner Child

Prompt 1:
If you could sit with the younger version of yourself right now, what would they look like? Picture their physical features and the essence of their being. What would they be wearing? Think about the colours, fabrics, and styles that express their spirit. What's the expression on their face? Is it one of joy, sadness, confusion, or longing?

Prompt 2:
Reflect on a specific memory where you felt scared, rejected, or unheard. Allow yourself to be vulnerable and recall every detail. What did you need in

that moment that you didn't receive? Were you longing for a comforting presence, a validating word, or perhaps just a simple hug?

Write a letter to that child, beginning with: "I see you. You didn't deserve that. I understand your pain, and I'm here to offer you the love and protection you need."

Section 2: Re-parenting Your Trauma Responses

Recognize that your triggers are not just random reactions; they are your inner child pleading, "Am I safe?" Re-parenting is about how you choose to respond to those triggers.

Use this template:

Trigger:
Identify a specific situation that made you spiral emotionally (e.g., feeling ignored by someone in a conversation).

Belief That Came Up:
Acknowledge the negative beliefs that surfaced during that moment. "I'm not important." / "I'm too much." / "They'll leave."

Response:
Reflect on how you reacted (e.g., shutting down, over-explaining, or people-pleasing).

Re-parenting Statement:
Counter those negative beliefs with positive affirmations: "You're allowed to have needs." "Not everyone will abandon you. I won't." "It's okay to feel scared. I've got you. I'm here to protect you."

Section 3: Coping Tools for CPTSD

Create a personal toolbox filled with techniques that resonate with you. Below are suggestions, tick or write what works for you:
Grounding
- 5-4-3-2-1 sensory scan
- Feet on the floor, hands over your heart
- Ice cube or cold water pressed against your skin

Journaling

- Write to your inner child, unleashing all that you want to say
- Track triggers and patterns to understand yourself better
- Gratitude lists, focus on three small wins each day

Soothing

- Curate music that calms or comforts you
- Use a weighted blanket for grounding
- Create and repeat positive affirmations to uplift your spirit (see below)

Section 4: Affirmations for the Inner Child

Stand in front of a mirror, repeat these affirmations out loud, or write them in your own handwriting to reinforce their power:
I am safe now."
- "It wasn't my fault."
- "I don't have to perform to be loved."
- "I choose to protect myself with compassion, not control."
- "I'm not a burden. I'm healing."

Create your own affirmation: "I am…" and fill in the blank with a statement that speaks to your strength and resilience.

Section 5: Visual Healing

Select a photo of yourself as a child, paste or draw it in your journal. Surround it with words, colours, or drawings that embody the safety, love, and warmth that you missed. Title this piece: "This Is Who I'm Healing for."

Personal Reflection: Healing the Inner Child – A Workbook for CPTSD Recovery

I didn't realize just how much I was carrying within me—the younger versions of myself.

There was the child who flinched at the sound of raised voices. The one who sought perfection in hopes of keeping loved ones close. The one who wore a smile to maintain peace, all while fighting back tears in silence.

These parts of me were still present, surfacing in my overreactions, my deep-seated fears of abandonment, and my tendency to shut down emotionally. Burnout didn't stem solely from work or life's responsibilities; it was rooted in a lifetime of emotional over functioning, where I felt the weight of adulthood long before experiencing the joys of childhood.

This section is meant for those young parts of you, the ones that never received the chance to rest, the ones still holding onto the belief that love must be earned.

Consider this your starting point; let it mark the beginning of a gentle journey toward self-discovery. May this be the moment you meet yourself with the warmth and kindness you have always needed.

Section 1: Meet Your Inner Child

Prompt 1:

- Take a moment to envision the child you once were.
- What do they look like?
- What are they wearing?
- What do their eyes convey?
- Describe them with the tenderness they deserve.

Prompt 2:

- Think back to a moment in your childhood when you felt unnoticed or unsafe.
- Now, write a letter to that child, starting with:
- "I see you. You didn't deserve that…"
- Tell them everything they needed to hear. Be the compassionate figure they wished for.

Section 2: Re-parenting Your Trauma Responses

Template for Awareness and Healing:
- Trigger: What situation stirred up a strong emotional reaction?
- Belief: What narrative surfaced? ("I'm too much." "They'll leave me.")

- Response: How did you respond? (Shutting down, seeking to please others, or expressing anger.)

Re-parenting Statement:

Speak to yourself with the same care and understanding you would offer a frightened child.
- "You are safe now."
- "Your needs matter."
- "It's okay to be upset—I'm here with you."

This gentle practice can be a powerful step toward healing and self-acceptance.

Section 3: Coping Tools for CPTSD

Take a moment to reflect on what resonates with you. You can tick what helps or jot down your own ideas:
- Engage in the 5-4-3-2-1 sensory grounding exercise.
- Try holding an ice cube or a cool cloth to soothe your senses.
- Write a letter to your inner child, offering them comfort.
- Listen to soft music that wraps you in a sense of safety.
- Remind yourself aloud: "I survived. I'm healing."

Soothing Ideas:
- Consider the embrace of a weighted blanket.
- Treat yourself to a warm bath by candlelight.
- Take nature walks without the distraction of your phone, simply being present.
- Create affirmation cards that speak directly to your heart.

Section 4: Affirmations for the Inner Child

Allow yourself to connect with these affirmations, speak them, whisper them, write them down, or tape them to your mirror:
- "I am safe now."
- "It wasn't my fault."
- "I don't have to earn love."
- "I am not a burden, I am healing."
- "I choose compassion over control."

- Feel free to add your own:
- I am... _____

Section 5: Visual Healing

- Find a cherished photo of yourself as a child, or create your own drawing.
- Surround it with all the love, safety, and warmth you needed back then.
- Use colours, doodles, or words of affirmation to express that love.
- Title it: "This Is Who I'm Healing for."

Final Reflection Prompt: Re-

- Reflect on the parts of your past that are asking for rest now.
- What would your younger self say if they saw how weary you feel?
- Respond to them gently and with care.
- Share with them what steps you're taking to ensure their safety now.
- Remember, you are no longer in survival mode; you have the right to rest.

Let this be a chapter where you stop running and begin to gently come home to yourself.

Check-In: How Are You, Really?

Before you move on, take a moment for yourself.
Place a hand gently on your chest or over your heart.
If it feels comfortable, close your eyes and take a deep breath.

Now, ask yourself:
"How am I, really, in this moment?"

Remember, there's no need to rush or to fix anything.
You don't have to put on a show for anyone.
Just take a moment to notice how you feel.

Are you feeling tense, tired, numb, or perhaps anxious?
Are you craving connection, a bit of rest, or just a moment of peace?

Whatever emotions or sensations arise, allow yourself to acknowledge them without judgment.
Let them be seen, felt, and truly yours.

This journey isn't a competition.
You have the freedom to pause, to breathe, to return later, or to simply stay here for a little while longer.

Believe it or not, you're doing better than you may realize.

And right now, that is more than enough.

Gentle Tools for Self-Compassion

Write to your inner child using their name or nickname (if you remember it). Begin with: *"I'm here now, and I see you."* Let the words come from a place of comfort, not correction.

Create a "safety box" filled with small items your inner child would have loved soft fabrics, calming scents, stickers, toys, or handwritten affirmations. Let this box be a tangible reminder of the care you now offer yourself.

Speak aloud one sentence of protection:

"You didn't deserve what happened. It's not your fault. I will protect you now."

Reflection Prompt

If you could go back and sit beside your younger self during their hardest moment, what would you say?

What did they most need to hear—but never did?

When you're ready turn the page to the next chapter.

Learning to Love Safely – Building Relationships After Trauma

Opening your heart can be one of life's greatest challenges, especially when years of self-protection have shaped your worldview. When your past is filled with experiences of abandonment, mistreatment, or neglect, the notion of love can quickly morph from a source of joy into a landscape of fear. Intimacy, which should feel like a comforting embrace, instead appears as a daunting risk, while vulnerability seems to throw you into the path of potential harm.

This is the insidious nature of trauma; it rewires your brain to be on constant alert, making you prone to perceive threats even in the safest of environments. In moments of affection, the instinctive reaction is often to tense up and brace for impact.

How Trauma Shaped My Relationships

For a significant period, I found myself oscillating wildly between two extremes: I was either overly attached, clutching desperately to the ones I cared about, or emotionally detached, retreating at the first hint of closeness. Having no reference for what healthy relationships looked like, I was trapped in survival-based connections, fearing the very intimacy that I yearned for.

As I navigated these tumultuous feelings, debilitating thoughts plagued me constantly, such as:

- "What's wrong with me? Why do I get scared when someone shows me kindness?"
- "Why do I instinctively push people away, especially when they get close?"
- "Why do I consistently find myself drawn to those who belittle my worth?"

Gradually, I realized that my reactions stemmed not from a brokenness within me but from the echoes of past wounds that still resonated deeply in my psyche.

The Body Remembers

Even when safety surrounded me, I learned that my nervous system was still caught in a web of the past. An unanswered text could ignite the flames of my abandonment fears, sending my mind spiralling back to earlier, more painful times. A raised voice could evoke the unrelenting anxiety of childhood. Even a simple compliment would trigger suspicion, "What ulterior motive could they possibly have?"

This is the cruel irony of trauma: it hijacks your present, distorting it into the familiar patterns of a painful past.

Re-learning Connection

Healing from trauma within relationships is a complex process, but throughout the journey, I've gathered valuable insights:

1. Safety Isn't Just About Words—It's About Consistency

I began to place greater importance on how others made me feel rather than solely on what they articulated. Safe individuals aren't just talkers; they're consistent in their actions. They won't make you second-guess your worth or dismiss your feelings. They show up for you, even when it's challenging for them. This consistent presence and support create a solid foundation where I can thrive.

2. Boundaries Aren't Walls—They're Doors with Locks

For a long time, I conflated the concept of boundaries with meaning rejection. With time and self-reflection, I've come to understand that boundaries are not barriers but rather protective measures that allow for meaningful connection without losing myself. I've learned to express my needs without apology, saying things like:
- "I need a moment to myself."
- "That behaviour doesn't feel okay to me."
- "Can we revisit this topic once I've had time to process?"

Recognizing that I have the right to assert my boundaries empowers me immensely.

3. I Don't Have to Heal Alone

I once believed that I needed to achieve complete healing before I could engage in love or accept it from others. However, I've discovered that healing often flourishes within the context of relationships, whether with a friend, a partner, or even a therapist. The crucial element is to choose individuals who honour your past and allow you to feel your feelings rather than attempting to fix or shame you. Healthy relationships acknowledge pain without attempting to erase it; they assure you that it's safe to experience it.

Rewiring My Attachment Style

Living with CPTSD has often left me feeling anxious about love, or at times overly avoidant, if not both. Now, I am learning to:
- Sit with discomfort rather than flee from it, giving myself the space to feel.
- Embrace emotional intimacy without succumbing to panic.
- Request reassurance without feeling shameful or inadequate.
- Trust that not everyone in my life is a source of harm.

This growth signifies progress. It is love. It is the foundation of safety.

Healing Tools That Helped Me

Here are some practical tools and strategies that have assisted me in my healing journey:
- Journaling about triggers to process emotions in a constructive way instead of projecting them onto others.
- Clearly expressing my needs, even in moments of discomfort.
- Seeking consent during emotionally charged conversations.
- Checking in with my nervous system to assess my readiness before reacting.
- Recognizing when it's time to let go of people whose familiarity does not coincide with safety.

If You Struggle to Trust...

I want to remind you: your reactions stem from a profound and understandable place. You are not "too sensitive", you're a person who has experienced pain and still dares to open your heart to love. It is entirely possible to unlearn the chaos of your past. You can attract the calm love you've always deserved. Begin building safety first within yourself, and then with others.

Personal Reflection: Practical Tools for Gentle Self-Compassion

Learning to trust again, whether it's yourself, others, or the world around you can be akin to finding your footing after a long period of struggle. It's a journey that can feel tender, awkward, and occasionally painful. However, with time and a gentle intention, moving with grace once more can become not just possible, but a beautiful reality.

Here are a few compassionate tools that have helped me on my path toward emotional safety:

1: The "Relationship Radar" Exercise

Begin by creating two lists:
- Safe People: Think of those who honour your feelings and create space for your vulnerabilities, not just your strengths.
- Unsafe or Inconsistent People: Acknowledge who makes you feel uneasy. This isn't about placing blame; it's about becoming aware of your relational landscape.

Once you have your lists, take a moment to look for patterns. What qualities do your safe people share? What boundaries do you need to establish with those who leave you feeling drained?

2: Nervous System Check-In Before Reacting

When you find yourself triggered in a relationship, pause and ask yourself:
- What emotion am I feeling in my body right now?
- Is this reaction rooted in the present, or does it belong to something from my past?
- What can help me feel safe in this moment?

Sometimes, taking a moment to regulate your body can be the first important step before addressing the conflict at hand.

3: Reassurance Is Not Weakness

Create a list of 2–3 affirming phrases that you would love to hear when you're feeling overwhelmed or triggered. For example:

- "I'm not going anywhere; I'm here for you."
- "You are not too much for me; you are enough."
- "I love you, even when things get messy."

You might choose to write these down, repeat them to yourself, or share them with someone you trust. Let these words become your anchor in times of need.

4. Inner Dialogue Script

When fear or emotional withdrawal arises, consider speaking softly to yourself with affirmations like:

- "It's perfectly okay to desire closeness."
- "Not everyone will hurt me as some have in the past."
- "I am safe, and I truly deserve real, healthy love."

Remember, repetition is key. The more you nurture your nervous system with messages of safety, the more it can learn to trust those messages.

Reflection Prompt: The Relationship I Deserve

What does a safe relationship look and feel like to you? Consider not what you've settled for but rather what you truly deserve.

Take a moment now to envision what a truly safe and loving relationship looks like for you. Make a point to write from the perspective of your healed self, not your past experiences.
How do they sound? How do they respond when you're feeling triggered? Consider how you feel in their presence, do you feel calm, free, or understood?

Take this space to outline your vision for the love you now know you are worthy of.

When Old Wounds Feel New – Emotional Flashbacks & Nervous System Healing

Sometimes, it all begins with a single gaze, a fleeting look that carries weight. Or perhaps it's the silence instead, a profound absence that speaks volumes. A subtle shift in tone, a delayed response, a sigh that escapes louder than intended, these seemingly trivial moments can send me reeling. In an instant, my heart begins to race, my chest feels as though it's tightening under an invisible weight, and my thoughts scatter chaotically, each one pulling me in a different direction. I find myself wishing to vanish, yet I grapple with understanding why I feel this way.

This isn't an overreaction; it's an emotional flashback.

What's an Emotional Flashback?

Unlike the gripping, vivid re-enactments you might see in movies, emotional flashbacks are quiet, insidious forces that can dismantle my sense of stability. There's no clear image or storyline playing out, just an overwhelming surge of emotions that seem to surge from nowhere, triggered by something that appears minor at best. The truth is, I'm being drawn back into the emotional imprint of a time when I didn't feel secure. Suddenly, a younger version of myself re-emerges, overshadowing my adult self.

Take a client I interviewed I shall call him Jason, for example, an individual whose reaction was puzzling yet telling. Every time someone stood too close behind him, Jason would freeze in panic. It wasn't a deliberate reaction; he didn't consciously understand the source of his fear. Still, his body betrayed him, becoming tense and rigid, his eyes scanning the room nervously, his voice trembling with uncertainty. As we delved deeper, it became clear that Jason's reaction was rooted in his past. His father used to linger silently in doorways, his ominous presence a precursor to unpredictable outbursts. His nervous system had internalized that threat, remembering even when he was unwittingly oblivious to it.

What It Feels Like (For Me)

When I find myself engulfed in an emotional flashback, I'm no longer inhabiting my adult body; I feel diminutive and vulnerable, like a frightened

134

child once more. I begin to apologize for perceived faux pas, even when I haven't done anything wrong. I rehearse my responses in anxious loops, withdraw into myself, and sometimes cry for reasons that elude my understanding. One vivid instance stands out: I left a social gathering prematurely because someone's lack of an enthusiastic response felt like an emotional blow. In that moment, it seemed as though I had committed an unthinkable wrongdoing. I spent the night spiralling in shame, overthinking every interaction. The reality? The person was simply tired, nothing more. Yet, my nervous system interpreted their silence as abandonment, dragging me back into a past filled with echoes of neglect. It wasn't about the present moment; it was a haunting from my past.

Recognising the Flashback

To navigate these turbulent waters, I've taught myself the essential skill of pausing. I carefully check in with myself rather than being swept away by the flood of emotions. I ask myself crucial questions:
- Is this emotion tied to the present or does it originate from the past?
- Am I experiencing a reaction that feels excessively hurt or panicked?
- Do I feel like a child grappling with adult realities right now?

Consider Liam, a close friend, whose fury would surface when he felt ignored in group chats. His devastation was not a mere matter of irritation; it was a profound emotional response. He lived under the assumption that he was "needy" until we uncovered that he was reliving the emotional neglect he faced as a child, where his cries for attention met silence. These emotional flashbacks often mask themselves as overreactions, but they are, in truth, understood reactions to past wounds.

Regulating My Nervous System

In the midst of an emotional flashback, logic frequently escapes me, not at first, anyway. My body requires reassurance before my mind can regain clarity. I return to the fundamentals of self-soothing:

Grounding:

- I anchor myself by naming the objects surrounding me.
- I seek the soothing chill of something cold in my hand.
- I remind myself aloud, "I'm here. I'm safe."

Movement:

- I shake my hands vigour-like, as if shaking off excess water.
- Walking barefoot on grass or engaging in slow, deliberate stretches often helps me reconnect with my body.
- I focus on breathing into the areas that feel restricted or tense.

Breath work:

- I count my breaths: inhaling for a count of four, holding, exhaling for another four, and pausing again.
- I strive for a longer exhale than inhale as a means of releasing pent-up energy.
- Sometimes, a dramatic sigh is all I need to feel a shift.

Re-Parenting Through Flashbacks

When I feel that child-like terror surging within me, I consciously choose to speak to myself in the gentle, nurturing way I always needed from others in those moments:

- "You're safe now."
- "This isn't your fault."
- "Love doesn't have to be earned."
- "I'm not leaving you."

Creating Safety in Everyday Life

True healing isn't solely about navigating emotional flashbacks; it's about fostering an existence where safety is the norm, not the exception. For me, that entails:

- Curating a calm playlist that replaces the chaos of news.
- Lighting a candle during moments of journaling and reflection.
- Dedication to digital detox days free from the incessant scroll.
- Practicing the power of "no" more often, prioritizing my emotional well-being.
- Surrounding myself with individuals who encourage my nervous system to exhale rather than tense up.

If This Is You Right Now…Please hear me:

You are not broken.
You are simply unearthing memories without possessing the full picture.
Your body communicates in a long-ago learned language—one rooted
deeply in survival.

But remember this you are now the adult. You possess the power of choice.
You can gradually learn the language of safety, softness, and compassion.
It's a gentle journey, taken one moment at a time.

Reflection Prompt: What Does Safety Feel Like?

Take a moment to close your eyes and envision a moment, whether real or
imagined, where you felt utterly safe. Where were you? What did you hear,
smell, see, and feel in that moment?

Write down:
What safety looks like to you.
What safety feels like in your body and soul.
How you can invite more of that feeling into your everyday life.

And if you can't yet conjure an image of safety, that's perfectly okay. Begin
by identifying what doesn't feel safe. This contrast can still guide you toward
understanding and, ultimately, healing.

Trusting Myself Again – Reclaiming Inner Authority After Trauma

There was a time when I found myself second-guessing everything in my life. Every decision weighed heavily on my mind, every thought seemed clouded, and every feeling was uncertain. It was as if fear and truth had become indistinguishable, wrapped in a haze of self-doubt and anxiety. That's the insidious impact of trauma, it scrambles your internal compass, leaving you adrift in a sea of uncertainty.

In the wake of past hurts, I learned to distrust my own instincts, the very instincts that should guide me. Moments that once felt clear became murky. I began to scan the room intently, gauging the reactions of others before I dared to listen to my own inner voice. I turned to friends and family for validation, asking for their opinions on decisions both trivial and significant, because my own judgment had begun to feel elusive and unsafe. My intuition, once a reliable ally, became silenced, its cries for attention drowned out by the cacophony of doubt.

Over time, I completely lost touch with what my own voice sounded like.

What It Feels Like to Lose Self-Trust

For me, losing that crucial trust in myself manifested in numerous unsettling ways:

I found myself apologizing incessantly, even in situations where I had done nothing wrong, a shadow of guilt hovering over me at all times.
I developed a relentless need for reassurance, seeking approval for every decision, no matter how minor, as if my ability to choose had been stripped away.
I became trapped in a loop of over-analysis, dissecting texts, conversations, and silences, deeply afraid of missteps that would confirm my fears of inadequacy.
Even the simplest choices, like what to eat for dinner, became paralyzing decisions that often left me feeling helpless.
I sought validation from others regarding my pain, questioning whether my feelings were legitimate, as doubt gnawed at my sense of reality.

139

And perhaps most unsettling of all, it felt as if I had disconnected from my very own body. I floated through life from the neck up, caught in a whirlwind of analysis yet devoid of genuine emotion.

Why It Happens

The roots of this self-doubt often lie in a childhood marked by gas lighting, invalidation, or neglect. When your reality is consistently denied, the world starts to feel unsafe. If you expressed sadness, you were told you were overreacting. Demonstrating anger led to punishment, and showing fear resulted in mockery. Any needs you had were labelled as excessive or burdensome. This relentless invalidation taught me to silence my feelings, eroding my ability to believe in my own perceptions. Gradually, I stopped trusting myself altogether, and ultimately, I ceased to choose myself. It wasn't a sign of weakness; it was a desperate act of self-preservation.

How I'm Rebuilding That Trust

Recognizing the need for healing meant making a pivotal promise to myself: I will stop abandoning who I am in the pursuit of safety. This journey to reclaim my self-trust began quietly, often feeling almost imperceptible at first, but with each step, I started to rebuild my relationship with myself.

1, I Started Writing Things Down

When my mind betrayed me, my journal became a steadfast ally. I poured out my thoughts and feelings onto the pages, no matter how confusing they seemed. Over time, I was able to look back and affirm, "See? You were right to feel that way." Documenting my experiences became a vital tool for clarity and validation.

2. I Tuned into My Body

Our bodies hold memories that our minds often overlook. I began to pay closer attention and asked myself questions like, "Where in my body do I feel this emotion?" and "What does my body truly need right now? Am I hungry, tired, anxious, or merely overstimulated?" As I listened more intently, I began to recognize patterns that provided insight, allowing me to trust the signals my body was sending.

3. I Practised Making Decisions Alone

140

I realized that not every decision needed to be perfect or validated by someone else. I started making low-stakes choices, what to wear, what to eat, when to take a break without seeking anyone's approval. Each time I chose for myself, I reaffirmed the belief that I am allowed to lead my own life, and each action became a small victory in reclaiming my autonomy.

4. I Let My Voice Be Heard

Even when my voice trembled or when others disagreed with me, I made the conscious decision to share my thoughts and opinions. I learned that my voice deserved to be heard, even if it wasn't polished or perfectly articulated. Speaking up, regardless of the outcome, became a powerful act of self-affirmation.

Learning to Have My Own Back

Ultimately, that's what true trust is, it's not about being correct all the time or having everything neatly figured out. It's about knowing that no matter what unfolds, I will stand by myself rather than turn inwardly against myself. Now, when I stumble or make mistakes, I remind myself:

"It's okay. We're still learning."
"You didn't betray yourself, you were just frightened."
"You're safe with me. I've got us."

Slowly but surely, I'm reconnecting with that inner voice, the one I used to silence. It's becoming my guide once more, leading me towards a path of self-acceptance and love.

Personal Reflection: Practical Tools for Gentle Self-Compassion

Reclaiming self-trust after experiencing trauma isn't just a one-time event; it's a journey filled with quiet, courageous moments where you consciously choose to believe in yourself again. If this chapter has touched something within you, consider it an early sign of healing. You're not behind, broken, or late, you're on a path of returning to your true self.

Here are a few gentle tools to help rebuild your inner authority with compassion and kindness:

1. *Create a "Self-Validation" Log*

Each time you experience a strong emotion, whether it's hurt, discomfort, joy, or confusion, take a moment to write it down. Avoid dissecting it; simply record how you feel. Over time, you'll begin to observe patterns that affirm your inner wisdom, helping you to see that your feelings are real and deserving of recognition.

2. *Mirror Talk – Affirming Your Inner Guide*

Every morning, take a moment to look into the mirror and speak to yourself the way you would to someone you love deeply. Use affirming phrases such as:
- "I trust your heart."
- "You've endured so much, yet you still care, and that truly matters."
- "You don't need to earn the right to exist just as you are."
- Let your reflection become a haven of safety rather than a space for judgment.

3. *"Small Decisions" Challenge*

Each day, try to make one small choice on your own, free from the influence of others. It could be what to wear, what music to enjoy, or what to eat. After making your decision, take a moment to affirm yourself:
"I made that choice, and I'm proud of it."
This practice helps cultivate a sense of internal safety over time, reminding you that your voice and preferences matter, even in the smallest of ways.

4. *Notice the "Self-Betrayal" Alarm*

When you feel discomfort, perhaps a tightness in your chest or a sinking feeling in your stomach, or if you find yourself wanting to apologize for simply existing, take a pause. This is your body signalling that you are drifting away from yourself. Gently place a hand over your heart and ask, "What do I need right now to feel safe with myself?"

5. *Write a Letter to the You Who Didn't Know Better*

142

This isn't about placing blame; it's about showing tenderness. Write a letter to the version of yourself who struggled with self-doubt, remained silent, or felt trapped. Assure them:

"You were simply trying to survive."

That version of you was never weak; they just lacked protection. Now, you have the beautiful opportunity to offer them the love and compassion they didn't receive back then.

Reflection Prompts

Think of a time you instinctively knew something, yet failed to trust yourself. What unfolded in that moment? How can you begin to honour that intuitive part of yourself moving forward?

Reflect on a time when you instinctively knew something was right, but you didn't trust yourself. What happened in that moment? How can you begin to honour that intuitive part of yourself as you move forward?

Boundaries and Self-Worth – Choosing Myself Without Apology

For a long time, I held a misconception: I believed that setting boundaries was synonymous with being selfish. Saying "no" felt like an admission of failure, a betrayal of those who relied on me. I thought that prioritizing my own needs meant I was akin to cold, detached individuals, those who tread on others for their own gain. However, I eventually realized that this behaviour wasn't true selflessness; it was rooted in fear and lingering trauma.

Somewhere along my journey, I had absorbed the notion that love equated to sacrifice. To be regarded as a "good" person meant I had to be perpetually available, agreeable, and quiet, even when every fibre of my being was in turmoil. In my efforts to be perceived as loving and accommodating, I lost a vital part of myself.

What a Lack of Boundaries Looked Like (For Me)

My experience with blurred boundaries manifested in several ways:
- I often said "yes" when deep down I really wanted to say "no," betraying my own feelings.
- I found myself explaining my thoughts to people who showed no interest in understanding.
- I allowed others to interrupt me, disrespect my opinions, and take advantage of my kindness.
- I felt an intrinsic responsibility for the emotions of everyone around me, believing their happiness was my burden to carry.
- I struggled with guilt whenever I took time to rest, chose to decline an invitation, or expressed a need that diverged from the wants of others.

And when I attempted to assert myself? My responses were often accompanied by excessive explanations, apologies, or a complete retreat back into silence. It became evident that I didn't believe I was entitled to take up space in conversations or relationships.

Where It Came From

The roots of this struggle can often be traced back to early experiences that taught me love was conditional. I learned to shape-shift into whoever I thought was required to keep me safe, seen, or accepted. My ability to scan the emotional landscape of the room meant I suppressed my own feelings in the process. Eventually, I reached a point where I could hardly recognize my own identity.

This is the perilous path of growing up without clear boundaries: the lines blur, and you lose the ability to discern where others end and you begin.

How I Started Reclaiming Myself

The journey to healing required the profound realization that I could let others down without compromising my worth. I discovered that prioritizing myself did not equate to cruelty; that cultivating peace within myself didn't need to come with a request for permission.

I Started Small

I didn't kick off this transformative journey with bold declarations of "no." Instead, I began with gentle, yet firm statements like:
- "Let me think about that and get back to you."
- "That doesn't align with my current priorities."
- "I'm not able to take that on right now."

Admittedly, this was a daunting exercise at first. However, with each moment I honoured my boundaries, I felt a part of myself soften. I was finally choosing myself.

I Defined What I Would No Longer Accept

To solidify this newfound understanding, I put pen to paper, writing down what I would no longer tolerate, not for anyone else's sake, but solely for myself. I committed to:
- Refusing to explain my trauma to those who dismiss it.
- Rejecting the idea of maintaining peace at the expense of my mental health.
- Saying "no" because I wanted to, not because I was afraid.

- No longer feeling the need to apologize for safeguarding my emotional energy.

These declarations transformed into my personal rules, gradually evolving into my unwavering standards.

I Connected Boundaries to Self-Worth

I came to understand that boundaries are not barriers erected to isolate others; rather, they are doors that I choose whether or not to open. They reflect acts of self-love and assert: "I matter too."

When You Start to Change...

It's important to recognize that change doesn't always resonate well with others. Those who previously benefitted from my lack of boundaries may resist the shift. Some might label me as distant or difficult, misinterpreting my newfound assertiveness.

But at the end of the day, my peace is non-negotiable. I owe no one an explanation for my silence, nor do I owe everyone access to my life. To be whole, I don't need to be liked by all.

Say It with Me:

"I am not responsible for how others feel about my boundary."
"I can say no without guilt, and I can say yes without fear."
"Every time I choose to honour myself, I draw closer to becoming my safest self."

Reflection Prompt:

What boundary have you hesitated to set, fearing the reaction it may provoke? Take a moment to visualize what it would feel like to finally honour that boundary, and how it could reshape your sense of self and well-being.

Personal Reflection: Gentle Tools for Nurturing Self-Compassion

Setting boundaries can often feel daunting. It's not just about saying no; it's about embracing the importance of saying yes to yourself. If you've devoted years to prioritizing others, the shift towards choosing your own needs may feel uncomfortable and even leave you with feelings of guilt. Yet, it's essential to recognize that your needs are valid, your limits matter, and your inner peace deserves protection.

Here are some gentle tools designed to help you affirm your boundaries and nurture your self-worth from within:

The "Guilt-Free No" Practice

Consider creating a list of gentle responses that allow you to decline without feeling the need to apologize or justify your decisions. Keep this list somewhere you can see it regularly. You might use phrases like:
"That doesn't work for me."
"I'm focusing on my own well-being right now."
"I need to honour my energy today."
These phrases aren't barriers; they're reflections of your true self.

Boundary Letters (That You Don't Have to Send)

Take a moment to write a letter to someone with whom you've felt challenged to set boundaries. Allow yourself to be honest, raw, and unapologetic. Express what you truly need, this is for you, not for them. The simple act of writing can be profoundly empowering, serving as a way to reclaim your voice.

Mirror Affirmations for Self-Worth

Stand in front of the mirror and speak these truths aloud:
"My needs are not a burden."
"It is not selfish to protect my peace."
"I am allowed to disappoint others without abandoning myself."
Let these affirmations serve as a comforting anchor when feelings of guilt or fear arise.

Your Non-Negotiables List

Reflect on what truly matters to you and identify your personal non-negotiables, your emotional deal breakers and must-haves. Write these down, as they represent the boundaries that safeguard your peace. Revisit this list regularly; it's not meant to shut others out, but to keep you grounded and steady.

Rest Without Earning It

Allow yourself the grace to simply be, practicing the art of doing nothing without guilt. Embrace saying no without the need for justification, and exist without the pressure of performance. By doing this, you begin to teach your nervous system that it's safe to stop over giving and to start receiving, especially from yourself.

Reflection Prompt:

Is there a particular boundary you've found difficult to establish, perhaps out of fear of the reaction it may evoke? Take a moment to visualize what it might feel like to honour that boundary. Consider how this choice could positively reshape your sense of self and enhance your overall well-being. Remember, your journey towards self-compassion is yours, and it deserves to be nurtured.

Shame, Guilt & Letting Go of What Was Never Yours

There are emotions that scream at us, loud and insistent and then there are those that quietly whisper in the shadows of our minds. Shame and guilt often evade our notice, slinking in without fanfare. They can exist like a dull ache deep in your chest, a relentless voice inside your head saying, "This was your fault."

You carry these burdens in silence, woven into the fabric of your being, because somewhere along the path of life, you were conditioned to believe that you deserved what transpired. That your pain rendered you difficult to love. That your truth was a burden to others. That if you had somehow been a better version of yourself, none of this anguish would have taken place. This is the insidious lie that trauma leaves in its wake, an untruth that festers and grows, entwining itself around your heart.

It's time to unlearn that lie.

Understanding the Difference

Guilt and shame are often intertwined yet represent very different emotional landscapes. Guilt whispers, "I did something wrong." It usually has a constructive role, guiding our moral compass and reminding us of our shared values. However, the guilt that arises from trauma is a twisted reflection of this, an insidious force that convinces us that we are to blame for the unthinkable actions taken against us.

On the other hand, shame is a more pervasive, gnawing presence. It digs deeper, embedding itself within our physical and emotional selves. It tells us we are unlovable, unworthy, and irretrievably broken. Shame can be one of the most toxic legacies we carry from experiences of trauma.

What It Looked Like for Me

For me, living under the weight of shame manifested in various forms:

151

- Apologizing for my existence as if simply being was an inconvenience to others.
- Shouldering the burden of responsibility for the choices made by those around me.
- Hiding parts of my authentic self in a desperate bid to become more "acceptable" to those who surrounded me.
- Believing my emotions were an inconvenience, a nuisance that only burdened others.
- Feeling I had to earn love through an endless cycle of over giving and neglecting my own needs.

And beneath it all lay a quiet yet heavy conviction: if people genuinely knew me, they would inevitably walk away.

Where Shame Comes From

It's crucial to recognize that shame doesn't arise from our true selves. Instead, it is cultivated through a toxic mixture of external messages and experiences. Shame can stem from:
- Being unjustly blamed for the actions and choices of others, bearing the emotional fallout that isn't ours to carry.
- Having our feelings dismissed or invalidated, further deepening the wound.
- Being told to simply "get over it," rather than being embraced and held through our pain.
- Carrying secrets that no child should ever be burdened with, secrets that stifle our voices.
- Feeling an overwhelming lack of safety when it comes to expressing emotions, crying, asking for help, or simply needing support.

We weren't born with shame; it was imparted to us through a myriad of experiences.

How I'm Learning to Let It Go

Releasing shame isn't a linear process, but here are some steps I've found helpful:

I Named It

Shame flourishes in the shadows of silence. By bringing it into the light and articulating it, I started to say, "That's shame talking," creating a barrier between me and the insidious voice that sought to diminish my worth.

I Gave It Context

Rather than fixating on the question, "What's wrong with me?", I shifted my focus to understanding the roots of my feelings: "Where did I learn to feel this way?" By doing so, the shame gradually transformed from something personal into a shared affliction, belonging to those who hurt me, to the systems that failed to protect me, and to a world that often doesn't understand how to love authentically.

I Spoke It Out Loud

I sought out safe spaces to articulate my feelings. Whether to a therapist, in a journal, or with someone who genuinely cared, sharing my experiences allowed me to release the hold shame had on me. The act of verbalizing it significantly diluted its power, revealing that shame cannot endure in the presence of empathy.

If You've Ever Thought, "It Was My Fault"

Let me be unequivocally clear: you were never responsible for your pain. You were never "too much." You were not weak for enduring the challenges life threw your way. What happened to you does not define who you are as a person. The measures you took to survive are not shameful; they are simply a testament to your resilience.

You do not have to carry the burden of what was never yours.

Personal Reflection: Embracing Gentle Self-Compassion

Healing from shame isn't about transforming into someone entirely different; rather, it's about reconnecting with the essence of who you truly are, long before the world imposed its expectations on you.

Shame flourishes in silence, secrecy, and harsh self-criticism. However, when you respond to it with kindness, understanding, and connection, you'll find it starts to lose its hold. The tools listed below are not quick solutions, they represent gentle acts of defiance against the belief that you are somehow unworthy.

Engage with Your Shame—Not from It

When shame speaks, it often echoes your own voice. Start to distinguish it from yourself by saying out loud:
"That thought doesn't belong to me."
"This narrative is outdated and not rooted in truth."
"I am safe to be exactly who I am."

If it helps, give shame a name. Approach it as you would a frightened child, lovingly yet confidently.

Nurture Your Younger Self

Visualize the version of you who first experienced the hurt of shame, whether that was at age 6 or 16. Write a letter to that younger self, conveying what they needed to hear the most:
"You were never to blame."
"I see how hard you tried."
"You didn't deserve what happened to you."

While you can't change the past, you can make a commitment to stop neglecting that part of yourself now.

Create a "Not Mine to Carry" List

Identify every heavy burden you've been shouldering, shame from someone else's actions, guilt over unmet expectations, silence around your pain. Next to each item, write:
"This was never mine to bear."

If it feels right, turn this into a ritual: tear it up, burn it safely, or bury it. Allow your body to participate in this release.

Journal Using These Prompts

- Where did I learn to believe I wasn't enough?
- What would shift if I released the shame for things that weren't my fault?

- What does freedom from guilt look, sound, and feel like in my body?

You may just uncover a well of wisdom within you once shame isn't dominating your thoughts.

Extend "Reverse Empathy"
Think of someone you love and imagine them sharing the story that you carry shame over, now as if it were their own. What would you say to comfort them?
And now, say those very words to yourself. Speak them aloud. You often extend deeper compassion to others than you do to yourself; it's time to shower yourself with that same kindness.

Reflection Prompt:

Consider this: What is one thing you have felt guilty or ashamed of over the years? Now, envision your younger self carrying that same heavy weight. What words of encouragement or understanding would you offer them to help lighten their load?

Take a moment to consider: What is one thing you've felt guilty or ashamed of throughout the years? Picture your younger self bearing that same heavy burden. What words of encouragement or understanding would you offer them to help lighten their load?

Becoming Me – Who Am I Without the Trauma?

For a long time, I felt adrift in a world that revolved around others' expectations, losing sight of my own identity.

I survived by adapting, moulding myself into whatever shape was needed in any given moment. I learned to be the quiet listener when someone needed comfort, the compliant friend who offered support without question, the strong figure who people relied on, and the helpful hand that never wavered. But if you asked me what my own desires were, what truly made my heart race with excitement, or who I was when the façade slipped away, I would find myself silent and uncertain.

For years, the weight of trauma overshadowed my individuality, drowning out my own voice amidst the cacophony of survival strategies. Living in a constant state of fight, flight, freeze, or fawn, I constructed my identity around survival mechanisms rather than a true sense of self. I became the people pleaser, the relentless hyper achiever, the emotional caretaker, the quiet isolator, and the fixer desperately trying to mend the cracks in others. I wasn't living my truth; I was merely conforming to the roles that others needed me to play.

And as I began to confront that trauma, I found myself grappling with an unsettling emptiness, a daunting question loomed over me like a shadow: Who am I if I'm no longer in survival mode?

Letting Go of False Selves

Throughout my journey, I encountered various versions of myself, each crafted as a defence mechanism. There was the version that smiled through ceilings of pain, the one that diminished her presence to feel safe, and the one who apologized for merely existing in spaces that often felt hostile. I owe these versions my gratitude; they kept me alive during tumultuous times. But as I grew and started to heal, I recognized that these masks no longer served me. I wanted, no, needed more than mere survival; I craved authenticity, truth, and a deeper connection to myself.

Reclaiming Myself, One Layer at a Time

I Gave Myself Permission to Be Curious

I embarked on a journey of self-discovery, asking myself profound questions: What brings me joy? What ignites a spark within me, not just fleeting moments of comfort? What are my true values? those that resonate with my essence rather than those imposed upon me by society or upbringing? Embracing the freedom to explore, to try new things, and even to fail, I learned to prioritize the journey of self-discovery over the relentless pursuit of perfection.

I Redefined Strength

I grew to understand that true strength isn't about never breaking down; it's about recognizing that I possess the resilience to rebuild myself, time and again. My understanding of strength evolved: it now manifests as the courage to speak up even when my voice trembles, the ability to say "no" without feeling guilt or shame, and the willingness to experience the full spectrum of my emotions while still choosing softness and compassion.

I Built a Life That Feels Like Home

Creating a sense of home became essential, not just in the physical spaces I inhabited but within myself. I stopped fighting for acceptance in places that made me feel small and insignificant. Instead, I focused on cultivating peace within. I dedicated time to embrace joy, to slow down, and to nurture authentic connections that honoured who I truly am.

If You're Still Figuring It Out...

That's perfectly okay. You don't need to have a meticulously crafted five-year plan or a flawless image of who you should be. What matters is your presence in the moment. Cultivate a willingness to explore, and extend gentleness toward yourself as you navigate this journey. You are not defined by the traumas that have shaped your past; rather, you are defined by who you choose to become in the process of healing.

You are not broken; you are in a beautiful state of unfolding, each layer revealing more of your true self.

Personal Reflection: Practical Tools for Gentle Self-Compassion

Rebuilding your identity after trauma is not about crafting an entirely new version of yourself. It's about gently rediscovering the parts of you that may have been overshadowed by the need to survive. This journey can be slow and often feels messy. But with each moment you choose curiosity over fear, softness over shame, and authenticity over performance, you're finding your way back to yourself.

Here are some practical tools that can support you on this heartfelt journey:

The "Who Am I Becoming?" Journal

Instead of asking, "Who am I?", which can seem daunting, consider exploring:
"Who am I learning to become?"
"What parts of me feel most like home?"
"What do I want to feel more of in my life?"
Allow your answers to unfold naturally. It's okay not to have everything figured out; what matters is that you remain engaged in a loving and honest dialogue with yourself.

Try Something You've Never Done—Just Because

Healing often reignites our sense of curiosity. Consider trying out activities like painting, hiking, learning a new language, or even dancing around your kitchen, whatever sparks joy within you. Ask yourself: "If I didn't have to be good at it, what would I truly love to try?" Embrace joy as part of who you are, not just as a by-product of productivity.

Mirror Check-Ins: Identity Without Armour

Once a week, take a moment to stand in front of a mirror and ask yourself:
"What part of me did I honour this week?"
"Where did I show up as my true self?"
"Where did I still hold back and why?"

Approach these questions with tenderness, not judgment. You're not tracking progress; you're simply tuning into your inner self.

Build a "Self-Home" Ritual

Create a sacred moment each week (or even daily) that feels uniquely yours. This could be as simple as lighting a candle to read, taking a walk to music that lifts your spirit, or cooking a favourite meal without any distractions. Let these rituals affirm to yourself: "I belong to myself. I am safe here."

Affirmations for Reclaiming Identity

Consider speaking these affirmations aloud, writing them in your journal, or placing them in visible spots:
"I am more than the person I had to become to survive."
"I deserve a life that feels authentically mine."
"I am not lost—I'm unfolding."

The essence of you that you seek is not a stranger; they are patiently awaiting your discovery beneath the layers of noise.

Reflection Prompt:

Take a moment to contemplate: if all fear, shame, and survival instincts were to dissolve, who would you be at your core?
What do you cherish deeply?
What ignites your curiosity?
What kind of life feels genuinely honest and fulfilling to you?

Healing in the Everyday – Mental Health Maintenance for Real Life

After navigating through countless breakdowns, breakthroughs, and moments of intense effort, I've come to an important realization: Healing doesn't always manifest as profound emotional disclosures or life-altering experiences. Often, it reveals itself in the simplicity of everyday actions.

Sometimes, healing looks like the mundane tasks we often overlook:
- Brushing your teeth, that small act of self-care.
- Drinking water, refreshing your body and mind.
- Saying no to the wrong people, setting boundaries that protect your energy.
- Stepping outside when your instinct is to retreat under the comfort of your duvet.

In truth, healing is rarely loud or dramatic. It seldom resembles poetry; instead, it resides in the incredibly ordinary—and therein lies its sacredness.

Why Maintenance Matters

Surviving a mental health crisis is a significant achievement, but it's only one part of the journey. The true challenge lies in staying anchored and balanced between those tumultuous waves. I discovered that when I shifted my focus from waiting for the inevitable low points to actively caring for myself on a regular basis, everything began to transform.

Mental health maintenance isn't about achieving perfection; it's about nurturing a continuous connection with yourself before you reach the edge of unravelling.

Daily Tools That Keep Me Anchored

Morning Check-In (No Phone First)

Before allowing the noise of the digital world to invade my mind, I take a moment to pause and ask myself:

- How do I truly feel right now?
- What do I need today, emotionally, physically, spiritually?
- What's one small gesture I can offer myself today, regardless of how chaotic the day might become?

Some mornings, my answers lead to enjoying tea and music that lift my spirits. On others, I may crave silence, tears, or movement. The triumph lies in the act of checking in with myself.

Movement That Feels Like Kindness

Movement shouldn't be synonymous with punishment or pressure; rather, it should embody kindness towards my own body. I embrace forms of movement that bring me joy, such as:
- Taking a leisurely walk without headphones, allowing nature to fill my senses.
- Stretching in bed, allowing my body to awaken gently.
- Dancing freely, as if no one is watching.
- Shaking off stress, like a wild animal instinctively resetting its nervous system.

My body craves permission to move, not the burden of discipline.

Food That Feels Grounding

Nourishment should not feel like a diet or a set of restrictions; it should come from a place of care. I frequently pause to ask myself:
- What would truly support and nourish my body right now?
- Am I eating out of hunger or emotion, and is it okay to feel that way today?
- I've learned not to moralize food; instead, I honour it as a vital part of my wellbeing.

Digital Boundaries

Screens can be overwhelming, particularly when I'm already feeling fragile. As a result, I've established some firm non-negotiables:
- No social media after 9 PM to give my mind a rest.
- Muting accounts that don't contribute positively to my mental state.
- Choosing slow, enriching content over chaotic noise.

163

- Replacing the temptation to doom scroll with journaling or listening to soothing music whenever possible.

The "Reset Hour"

Every day, I dedicate time just to be. This hour is free from expectations and goals, simply a space to reconnect with myself. Some days, this manifests as light cleaning; on others, it might involve crying or taking a nap. But no matter what I do, I always aim to return to my core self. Even just 15 minutes of intentional stillness can pull me back from the brink.

Mini-Affirmations

There are moments when I don't feel strong, but I've learned the power of self-affirmation. I remind myself:
"I'm allowed to rest."
"I'm doing better than I think."
"Even on my worst day, I am worthy."
"I can start over, right now."

Maintenance Is the Real Magic

The transformative moments in life aren't just the dramatic ones; they're found in the small, repeated gestures of care and commitment to ourselves. The more I engage with myself in these gentle ways, the more stable and resilient I feel when confronted with life's bigger challenges.

This journey isn't about achieving healing in one grand gesture; it's about nurturing ongoing healing day by day, softly, in ways that may go unnoticed by others but are always felt deeply within.

Reflection Prompt

What daily practice allows you to connect with your true self? Consider what gentle ritual you could introduce to your day—not as a task to check off, but as an act of love towards yourself.

Remember you are enough and you are worth it

The Setbacks Don't Erase the Progress – Learning to Fall Without Losing Yourself

No one told me that healing could encompass such a wide spectrum of emotions. It often feels like progress intertwined with panic, moments of genuine peace mixed with unexpected relapses. There are days when I reflect on how far I've come, only to suddenly question, "Why am I finding myself in this place again?"

In the past, I believed that a setback equated to failure. I thought that all the hard work I had put into my growth could be instantly undone by a single spiral into anxiety, an unexpected panic attack, or an emotional shutdown. But I've come to realize that I was mistaken. Setbacks don't signify that I'm broken; rather, they are a testament to my humanity.

The Truth About Healing

Healing is not a straight path; it's more accurately described as a circle, a spiral, or even a maze. There will be days when I feel like I'm soaring, days when I crash hard, and then there will be days when simply surviving the day becomes my greatest achievement. And you know what? That is perfectly okay. Growth isn't solely measured by how many steps forward I've taken but by how I choose to treat myself when I find myself taking steps back.

Why Setbacks Happen

Setbacks shouldn't be viewed as a sign that I'm doing something wrong. They are often just my nervous system trying to protect me in the only way it knows how. These setbacks frequently arise in situations like:

- Being unexpectedly triggered by an event or memory
- Experiencing exhaustion that leaves me emotionally vulnerable
- Confronting change, sometimes even the positive kind
- Letting go of my daily routines that provide stability
- Encountering reminders of my past that stir emotions I wasn't prepared to deal with

167

What Mine Looked Like

I have experienced moments where I snapped at someone I care for, only to be consumed by a wave of shame soon after. There were times I cancelled plans despite genuinely wanting to be there, only to find myself weighed down by feelings of isolation and self-loathing. I have felt the overwhelming urge to numb my emotions, to disappear entirely, thinking, "Maybe it's easier to succumb to old habits." In those moments, I found myself believing the false narrative that I hadn't changed at all.

But I've learned an important lesson: relapse does not equal failure; instead, it serves as feedback.

What I Do Now When I Slip

I Don't Punish Myself

In the past, I reacted to my pain with shame and self-criticism. Now, I choose to respond with presence and understanding. I ask myself important questions: "What is it that I really need right now?" "How can I offer myself comfort instead of judgment?" "What would I say to a dear friend if they were in my position?" And then I voice these affirmations to myself.

I Re-anchor

I return to the basics that ground me: Hydration, mindful breathing, journaling my thoughts, ensuring I get adequate rest, and naming my emotions rather than avoiding them. Just one of these actions helps restore my sense of control and stability.

I Track the Pattern, Not Just the Pain

Each relapse leaves behind a breadcrumb trail. I reflect on: What led up to this moment? What warning signs did I overlook? How can I adjust my approach in the future? My goal is to show up with more compassion and softness instead of succumbing to self-pressure. This shift allows me to transform feelings of shame into meaningful self-awareness.

I Remind Myself: I Am Still Healing

One difficult moment does not erase the countless brave steps I have taken before. Healing isn't about achieving a state of perfection or never falling again; it's about learning how to navigate those falls with a gentler landing and a greater sense of care for myself.

A Note for You (Yes, You)

If you find yourself reading this while mid-relapse, feeling overwhelmed and doubtful, I want to remind you of something crucial: You haven't ruined anything. You remain deserving of love and compassion. You haven't lost your progress; you might just be walking through a shadow. But the light is still present. So take a deep breath, reconnect with your true self, and remember, you're not behind. You are exactly where you need to be, right on time.

Reflection Prompt:

What's something you once perceived as a failure that you now recognize as a plea for care?

Gratitude, Growth & New Foundations

For a long time, my focus was solely on what was missing in my life. I was consumed by the fragmented parts of myself that remained unhealed, the emotional wounds that weighed heavily on my heart, and the habits I continued to struggle with. I would replay the days where I faltered, felt inadequate, or couldn't cope "well enough." I was fixated on the ideal version of myself that I had yet to fully become, and it left me feeling lost, almost in a perpetual state of comparison.

But then, somewhere along the journey, a shift began to occur within me. I `gradually learned to stop measuring my progress by an unattainable standard of perfection, and instead, I started to recognize and celebrate the quiet victories that had been happening all along. I noticed the significant, yet subtle, changes in my life—the deep breath I took before reacting in anger or frustration, the firm boundary I established without guilt or apology, the tear that fell but didn't carry shame. I began to cherish the moments I chose to prioritize rest and reflection rather than rushing forward. That realization marked true growth and a new understanding of healing.

The Gratitude I Didn't Know I Needed

At first, I believed that gratitude required grand gestures, creating elaborate vision boards or filling journals with radiant affirmations. However, I have come to understand that gratitude can be much quieter and more intimate. It manifests in the way I speak to myself in the mindful pauses I take before spiralling into negativity, and in the way I allow joy to enter my life, even when a part of me wrestles with feelings of unworthiness. I've realized that gratitude doesn't mean overlooking the pain; rather, it's about recognizing that pain did not define or destroy me.

Growth Looks Like This

Growth isn't always a relentless climb toward higher peaks; sometimes, it's about taking a moment to stay still, to root oneself deeply, and to ground oneself in the present rather than hastily running away from discomfort. For me, growth has meant several transformative realizations:
- Embracing vulnerability by admitting, "I don't know yet," without feeling ashamed.

- Gently reconstructing my routines with compassion and softness, instead of harshness and force.
- Letting go of relationships, places, and identities that no longer resonate with who I am becoming.
- Finding new meaning and purpose from previous pain, using it as a stepping stone rather than a stumbling block.

This healing process has gifted me a new foundation—one that isn't perfect or polished, but is truly solid and authentically mine.

Building New Foundations

There comes a pivotal moment in healing when the perspective shifts: you no longer focus solely on fixing what was broken, but you begin to build something entirely new from the ground up. This phase of transformation is sacred; it prompts deep questions that shape your life:
- What kind of life do I desire to create now?
- What do I genuinely believe at my core, not simply what I have been taught to believe?
- What can I fashion from all that I have reclaimed and rediscovered?

This new creation doesn't need to be monumental. Sometimes, growth is found in the simplest of things:
- Experiencing peace in the stillness of the morning.
- Waking up without the looming dread that once accompanied my thoughts.
- Looking into the mirror and feeling a sense of acceptance, maybe even love, instead of disdain.
- And that realization that sense of quiet contentment can mean everything.

What I'm Thankful for Now

I find gratitude for the pain that had to crack me open so that I could find the light within. I appreciate the moments of silence that urged me to listen inward and hear my own voice. I am thankful for the setbacks that forced me to slow down, creating spaces for necessary reflection. Above all, I am grateful for the courage that has allowed me to begin again, time and time again, even when the weight of the world felt unbearable.

Most importantly, I am thankful that I didn't give up on myself, even during the darkest moments when hope felt fleeting. Especially during those times, I clung to the belief that there was still a path forward.

Reflection Prompt:
What have you survived that, at one point, felt utterly impossible?
What part of your healing journey fills you with pride, no matter how small or seemingly insignificant?
And as you move forward, what kind of life would honour the depth of everything you've been through?

Closing Letter – From Me to You

Dear reader,

As you find yourself here, I encourage you to pause for a moment. Take a deep breath, inhaling the calm and exhaling the tension. Allow this realization to sink in: you have made it through so much. You've navigated not only the pages of this book but countless pivotal moments in your life that, at times, felt insurmountable. Yet, you are still standing, still here, what an incredible feat that is.

That alone speaks volumes about your strength and resilience.

Though I don't know the intricate details of your journey, the struggles you've faced, the burdens you've carried within, or the emotions you've kept hidden behind a façade of smiles, laughter, or silence. I want you to know something profoundly important: you are not defined by your past. You are not your diagnosis or your scars. You are not broken.

Instead, you are a person who has felt deeply, confronted challenges with bravery, and, against all odds, made the courageous choice to start anew. This is not a sign of weakness; it embodies a unique kind of strength that the world might not always recognize or appreciate.

If no one has reminded you of this today, let me do so now:

You have every right to take up space in this world. You deserve to rest, to recharge without guilt. Your voice matters, and you are entitled to speak your truth, however raw or complicated it may be. Healing is not a race; you can progress at your own pace, and you are genuinely worthy of the peace and joy you've been seeking for so long.

It's essential to remember that healing isn't merely a destination to reach; it's an evolving relationship with yourself. Some days will find you feeling strong and capable, while others may leave you feeling fragmented or lost. There will be times when you might forget the lessons you've learned along your journey, only to have those insights return to you in moments of need. And that's perfectly okay; it's part of this intricate process.

Healing is often messy, layered, and sacred. It unfolds in a non-linear fashion and is uniquely yours to navigate, no one else's journey can mirror yours.

I penned this book because I too have walked through those shadows. I know intimately the feeling of being utterly exhausted by the weight of my own thoughts. Yet, amidst that darkness, I also discovered the quiet joy of reconnecting with my true self, slowly, gently, and with honesty.

If you take away nothing else from these pages, please carry this truth with you: You are not alone. You have never been alone. No matter how many times you feel like you're falling apart, remember this: you always have the right to begin again.

With all my love and understanding,

Someone who truly gets it,

Healing Toolkit

You've embarked on a profound journey of self-discovery and healing. You've engaged deeply with stories of struggle and resilience, faced the complexities of your emotions, and acknowledged that healing is often a messy process, yet it is absolutely attainable.

This section serves as a refuge during those times when you feel overwhelmed, triggered, exhausted, or uncertain about your next steps. There's no need to revisit the entire text; instead, you can find solace and support right here. Take what resonates with you and leave behind what doesn't.

Daily Self Check-In Questions

Pause for a moment and reflect on these questions:
- What am I feeling right now? Recognizing your feelings is the first step toward understanding them.
- What does my body need today? Tune into your physical self; it often communicates what you might need.
- What emotion am I avoiding? Acknowledging avoided feelings can lead to breakthroughs in your healing.
- Where in my body am I holding tension? Identifying areas of tension can help you focus on releasing them.
- What's one kind thing I can say to myself right now? Self-compassion is crucial; nurture yourself with gentle words.

Grounding Techniques for Flashbacks or Anxiety

When you find yourself confronting overwhelming emotions, these techniques can be invaluable:
- 5-4-3-2-1 Scan: Ground yourself with your surroundings:
- 5 things you can see
- 4 things you can touch
- 3 things you can hear
- 2 things you can smell
- 1 thing you can taste

- Cold water or ice on your skin: This sensation can shock your nervous system back to the present moment and help you regain control.
- Weighted blanket, deep pressure, or firm touch: These can create a sense of safety and comfort for your body.
- Box breathing: A simple way to calm anxiety, inhale for 4 counts, hold for 4, exhale for 4, hold for 4, and repeat.

Re-parenting Statements

In moments of feeling unsafe, triggered, or diminished, remind yourself with these affirmations:
"You are safe now."
"This feeling is old; it is not dangerous."
"It's okay to rest. I'm here for you."
"You didn't do anything wrong."
"You're allowed to take up space in this world."

Journal Prompts by Topic

Engage with your thoughts through these prompts, tailored to specific feelings and experiences:

Anxiety:

- What narrative am I constructing about my current situation?
- What truths can I identify amidst the chaos?

Grief or Loss:

- What do I miss the most about what I've lost?
- What unspoken words or feelings do I need to express?

Trauma Reflection:

- What did I need during my traumatic experiences that I did not receive?
- How have I adapted to survive, and what can I start to let go of now?

Self-Worth:

- If I truly believed I was enough; what actions would I take today?
- Which part of myself is craving love and attention right now?

Favourite Affirmations

Affirmations can provide strength and comfort. Use these as they resonate with you, or create your own:
"I'm healing, even when it feels like I'm not."
"I don't have to be perfect to be worthy of love and acceptance."
"My boundaries are my right, and they matter."
"It's perfectly okay to have bad days; they don't define me."
"I am not defined by my past; I am becoming who I choose to be."

Return to this page whenever you feel lost or in doubt. Remember that you have travelled far on this path; you are actively engaged in the work of healing. You are not alone in this process, layer by layer, you are reclaiming your sense of self and moving toward wellness.

Bonus Section – Mental Health Resources & Helplines

You Don't Have to Heal Alone

It's important to remember that you don't have to navigate your mental health journey on your own. Whether you're in the middle of a crisis, looking for a qualified therapist, or simply need someone to listen, there are numerous individuals and services that genuinely care about your well-being, understand your struggles, and are ready to lend a hand.

Here's a comprehensive list of trusted mental health services available in the UK and internationally, along with self-guided platforms and supportive communities for your consideration.

UK-Based Helplines & Support Services

`Samaritans (24/7 Emotional Support)
☎ 116 123
🌐 Visit Samaritans www.samaritans.org.
Free and confidential support available for anyone in distress, day or night. No issue is too big or too small to speak about.

Mind
☎ 0300 123 3393
🌐 Visit Mind – www.mind.org.uk
Offers detailed information, guidance, and mental health support services to empower individuals to take control of their mental well-being.

SHOUT Crisis Text Line
📱 Text SHOUT to 85258
🌐 Give Us A Shout - https://giveusashout.org
A free, 24/7 text service providing immediate support to anyone in crisis—just text and connect with a trained crisis volunteer.

CALM (Campaign Against Living Miserably)
☎ 0800 58 58 58
🌐 Visit CALM - www.thecalmzone.net.

Dedicated to supporting men's mental health and tackling suicide prevention, providing a safe space to talk.

NHS Mental Health Services
🌐 Visit NHS Mental Health - www.nhs.uk
Access a variety of services, including IAPT (Improving Access to Psychological Therapies) and urgent support for those in need.

YoungMinds (Support for Young People and Parents)
📞 Parent Helpline: 0808 802 5544
🌐 Visit YoungMinds - www.youngminds.org.uk
Offers guidance and support specifically tailored for children, teenagers, and their parents, covering a multitude of mental health issues.

National Domestic Abuse Helpline
📞 0808 2000 247
🌐 Visit National Domestic Abuse Helpline - www.nationaldahelpline.org.uk
Provides 24-hour, confidential support for individuals experiencing domestic abuse, ensuring help is always available.

Cruse Bereavement Support
📞 0808 808 1677
🌐 Visit Cruse - www.cruse.org.uk
Offering compassionate support for anyone grappling with grief and loss, helping you through your difficult times.

International Resources

Mental Health America
🌐 Visit Mental Health America - https://mhanational.org/
A leading non-profit dedicated to helping all Americans achieve wellness by providing various resources and support.

Crisis Text Line (US/Canada)
📱 Text HOME to 741741
Offer immediate help via text messaging, connecting you to trained crisis counsellors.

International Suicide Prevention Directory
🌐 Visit Suicide Prevention Directory - https://befrienders.org/

A global directory to help locate crisis centres around the world for support in times of need.

The Trevor Project (LGBTQ+ Youth – US-based)
☎ 1-866-488-7386
🌐 Visit The Trevor Project - https://www.thetrevorproject.org/
Focused on crisis intervention and suicide prevention specifically for LGBTQ+ young people, providing dedicated support.

Self-Guided Tools & Therapy Apps

BetterHelp
Online therapy platform that connects you with licensed professionals for personalized support.

Headspace
Offers guided meditation and mindfulness techniques aimed at alleviating anxiety, enhancing sleep, and increasing focus.

Calm
Features breathwork, soothing sleep stories, and meditation resources to help you relax and find tranquillity.

Woebot
An AI-powered chatbot that provides emotional support techniques, helping you navigate your feelings in real-time.

Moodpath / MindDoc
Enables daily check-ins and tracks your mental health journey, promoting self-awareness and understanding.

Daylio
A mood tracker and micro-diary that helps capture your daily feelings and thoughts, aiding in reflection and emotional management.

Finding a Therapist

BACP (British Association for Counselling & Psychotherapy)
🌐 Visit BACP - https://www.bacp.co.uk
A professional body representing counsellors and psychotherapists in the UK, providing resources for finding qualified professionals.

Counselling Directory (UK)
🌐 Visit Counselling Directory - https://www.counselling-directory.org.uk
A comprehensive database of therapists across the UK, making it easier to find needed support.

Psychology Today (Global)
🌐 Visit Psychology Today - https://www.psychologytoday.com
A resource for locating therapists and psychological resources worldwide, tailored to your specific needs.

Final Reminder

Reaching out for support is not a sign of weakness; it is an incredible display of strength that many people struggle to exhibit. You don't have to wait until you're feeling overwhelmed or in crisis to seek assistance. Remember, mental health support is available for everyone, at any time.

Take this opportunity to save these important resources, share them with those who may benefit, and utilize them as needed. Healing can be a challenging journey, but you are not alone in this process. Together, support can make the difference.

About the Author / Your Ongoing Healing

Dear Reader,

My name is Josiah Cornell. I didn't write this book as a therapist. I didn't write it from some mountaintop of healing or as someone with all the answers.
I wrote it as someone who knows what it's like to sit in the silence of your own pain and wonder if anyone sees you.
I've been there, in the shadows, in the spiral, in the quiet moments where survival felt like the only thing I knew how to do.
And still, somehow, I chose to heal.
Not perfectly. Not all at once. But truthfully. Gently. And on my terms.

I've worked in HMPS Thameside and HMPS ISIS, with Havering probation services, in domestic violence support in Southend-on-Sea, and alongside people who have been ignored, dismissed, or forgotten.
I've trained in bereavement counselling, child and adult psychology, ADHD and autism support, and mental health awareness.
But none of that matters as much as this:
I've lived it.
The grief that lingers long after the funeral.
The shutdowns no one understood.
The shame that clings to your skin like smoke.
This isn't just a book.
It's a quiet, honest offering. A mirror for the parts of you that still ache.
A reflection of every person I've ever sat with who whispered,

"I don't know how much longer I can do this."

"Please give me a break"

And of the version of me who once whispered the same.

What I Believe

I believe trauma doesn't make you broken, it makes you real.
I believe healing doesn't look like a straight line; it looks like courage,
chaos, and coming back to yourself.
I believe your story matters, even if no one else has ever made you feel
that way.
And I believe, with no doubt in my heart, that you are worth every
breath, every pause, every ounce of care it takes to heal.

Your Healing Is Still Happening

You don't need to fix yourself.
You don't need to be further along.
You are already worthy, as you are, and as you are becoming.
Let this book be the hand you reach for when the world feels too
heavy.
Let it be your reminder:
You're not alone.
Someone gets it.
And if no one else says it today
I'm proud of you.

For surviving.
For feeling.
For not giving up on yourself.

You are already healing, simply by choosing to keep going.

Keep choosing you.
You deserve a life that doesn't just look okay on the outside, but feels like freedom on the inside.

With love, truth, and unwavering belief in you,

Josiah Cornell

Notes

Please make your own notes from this part of the book so you can refer back to them at any time.

www.ingramcontent.com/pod-product-compliance
Lightning Source LLC
Chambersburg PA
CBHW060422130626
46555CB00005B/2170